The Bootlegger's Other Daughter

—

NUMBER FOUR:
Sam Rayburn Series on Rural Life
Sponsored by Texas A&M University-Commerce
James A. Grimshaw, Jr., General Editor

The Bootlegger's Other Daughter

~

MARY CIMAROLLI

TEXAS A&M UNIVERSITY PRESS
COLLEGE STATION

The paper used in this book meets the minimum requirements
of the American National Standard for Permanence
of Paper for Printed Library Materials, z39.48-1984.
Binding materials have been chosen for durability.
∞

Library of Congress Cataloging-in-Publication Data

Cimarolli, Mary, 1931–
The bootlegger's other daughter / Mary Cimarolli.—1st ed.
p. cm. — (Sam Rayburn series on rural life ; no. 4)
Includes bibliographical references (p.) and index.
ISBN 1-58544-260-7 (cloth : alk. paper)
1. Cimarolli, Mary, 1931—Childhood and youth. 2. Texas, East—Social life
and customs. 3. Texas, East—Biography. I. Title. II. Series.
CT275.C595 A3 2003
976.4'14062'092—dc21
2002154911

In memory of Tice and Katie Gammill

and Sandy Brackeen

and for my sister, Lola Pearl Andree

CONTENTS

LIST OF ILLUSTRATIONS ix

SERIES EDITOR'S FOREWORD xi

ACKNOWLEDGMENTS xiii

PROLOGUE 3

Making Sense of My Senses 5

End of the Beginning 19

On Our Own 21

*Through the Eyes of
a Bootlegger's Daughter* 35

*Witnesses to the End of
the Nineteenth Century* 40

*Witnesses to the Beginning of
the Twentieth Century* 53

Living in a Wagon Shed 64

Guilt by Association 69

A Safe Haven 72

A Trilogy of Diversions 78

Cotton Stamps, Socks, and Self-Respect 92

Yellow Dogs, Politics, and Racism 98

"Risins" and "Rheumatiz" *104*

*Daddy Leaves Home to
Pick Cotton Out West* *109*

The Smell of Modernization *114*

Murder or Accident? *117*

Sounds of War *120*

*Of Sugar, Shoes, and
Other Wartime Shortages* *128*

Puberty and War *134*

Death Comes to Our House *139*

An Alien in My Own Country *144*

Conflicts of the Heart *150*

Leaving East Texas *158*

EPILOGUE 163

INDEX 169

ILLUSTRATIONS

Grandpa Tom Gammill and me (Mary Lou), circa 1933 6

Lola Pearl, J. T., and me on the farm at Arbala, circa 1935 7

Grandma Molly Gammill, circa 1941 44

Grandparents Lank and India Pearl, circa 1900 47

Great Grandmother Amanda Cates, circa 1890 49

My mama, Katie Lomax, circa 1920 51

My daddy, Tice Gammill, circa 1918 58

Tice Gammill and friend, circa 1920 59

Tice Gammill and friend, circa 1922 61

My school picture, Seymore School, circa 1938 73

My school picture, Seymore School, circa 1939–40 93

My school picture, Seymore School, circa 1941 125

Seymore School, 1942 126

Katie Lomax Gammill, circa 1942 130

J. T. Gammill, circa 1944 140

SERIES EDITOR'S FOREWORD

Established in 1997 under the umbrella of the Texas A&M University Press book publishing program, the Sam Rayburn Series on Rural Life focuses on facets of rural life in East Texas in particular and in Texas and the surrounding region in general. Subjects that may be addressed include, but are not limited to, banking, public education, literary figures, cotton, oil and gas, sports, higher education, little theater, politics, social work, history, art, and agriculture. The fourth title in this series, *The Bootlegger's Other Daughter,* adds another dimension, as a memoir that relates to many of the subjects listed above. Told in a Chaucerian style of the framing tale, the manuscript was originally titled "The Rustic's Tale: A Memoir." In it, Mary Cimarolli adds to her recollections "dialogues" with relatives and friends about place, time, and people.

Hometown Arbala, Texas, in the northeast part of the state, serves as a base from which memories begin, go back in time, and then go forward, ultimately covering the period from 1900 to 1990, although focusing on the Depression and war years. This charming tale begins with sensory perceptions from early childhood and admirable attention to the details of her surroundings, creating the mental images that allow the reader to be in that place with the teller of the tale. Names of products of the early twentieth century stir memories for those old enough to recognize them and perhaps stoke the curiosity of those who do not remember: Brogans, Prince Albert, Bull Durham, Black Draught, Burma Shave, and Vicks Salve. But Arbala is not the only setting of these memories.

Time dictated changes in place for the family or certain members of the family. The necessity of supporting a family during hard times and during two world wars took family members from northeast

Texas to West Texas and points in between, such as Dallas, Green-ville, and Commerce. The advent of the automobile (the Model-T Ford) and the railroad played significant roles in the family's lives and occupations. From farming and picking cotton to working on the railroad and working for Ford Motor Company, life shifted from ru-ral to urban over the years. And moonlighting jobs such as bootleg-ging during the Prohibition era and breeding mules during the Great Depression brought additional income and sometimes embarrass-ment for the family. None of these moments of revelation and con-fession is told sententiously. Cimarolli's style is engaging, at times humorous, and informative.

Life on the farm taught lessons not learned in urban settings. Hog killing time, for example, taught the economy of using all the parts, the importance of timing, and the value of sharing. People shared in other ways, too. Outdoor revival meetings, a typhoid fever outbreak, and cotton stamps brought people together in mixed and varied ways. And the larger figures of politicians, the FDR years, and familial re-lationships are intricately woven into this tale, which sees retrospec-tively beyond the county line. H. V. Kaltenborn, Edward R. Morrow, William Shirer, Ernie Pyle, and Bill Mauldin made their impressions. Colloquialisms, home remedies, Yellow-dog Democrats, and racism are also fair game for analysis. And ever present is the role of women throughout this period, among which was the role of teacher. Cima-rolli was wife, mother, widow, single parent, and wage earner, roles one discerns by the end of her memoir.

Cimarolli, a teacher herself, offers a variety of literary allusions that enhance this remarkable story: Dreiser, Wolfe, Twain, Dickin-son, and Frost are among the several mentioned. And parts of her story may remind one of the stories of others. The relationship be-tween siblings, the Graveyard Working Day, and the outdoor revival meetings are reminiscent of Clyde Edgerton's fiction, while the scene at the "seating-at-the-counter-only café" in Sulphur Springs brings to mind Robert Penn Warren's short story, "The Patented Gate and the Mean Hamburger." What we receive from this tale, then, is more than just one family's story, though we clearly have that, too. Cimarolli's graceful style, her eye for details, and her sensitivity to the larger pic-ture create a new snapshot with multiple dimensions in the Sam Ray-burn Series on Rural Life album. —JAMES A. GRIMSHAW, JR.

General Editor

ACKNOWLEDGMENTS

I am most grateful to Dr. James Grimshaw and the Sam Rayburn Series on Rural Life for their belief in this project; to my sister, Lola Andree, who helped me recall incidents I had forgotten; to the late Sandy Brackeen, who cheered me on all the way to the end; and to my husband, Jack Robottom, for his advice, support, and love.

The Bootlegger's Other Daughter

PROLOGUE

The period 1900–90 was witness to a transformation of humanity and human society without parallel in history. My parents' lives and, derivatively, mine commence with the turn of the century. Edward VII by the grace of God, King of Great Britain and Dominions beyond the Seas, Emperor of India, and so forth, had been crowned sovereign of that one quarter of the earth's land colored red.

Kaiser (Caesar) Wilhelm II was having his uniforms tailored to disguise his withered arm, and a failed Austrian painter was doing odd jobs in Vienna. Teddy Roosevelt was living the strenuous life in and out of the Bully Pulpit, and Lenin was an obscure revolutionary editing an equally obscure journal of opinion called, prophetically, *Iskra* (the spark).

My family's entrance into this century was unnoticed even in "the short and simple annals of the poor," as Thomas Gray has movingly called it. One smiles at the Providence that made them such improbable contemporaries of these historical personages.

In July of 1914, the era that had begun with the Stone Age was about to end. In August of 1914, modern western civilization began. One world came to an end—the new and unknowable and unseeable world commenced. In 1914 my mother was ten; my father was twelve. Their feet were firmly planted in two worlds without their knowing it.

AUTHOR'S NOTE

The recollections in this memoir, those of a child, are more vivid and accurate than those of my later years. A few names have been

altered, perhaps from a country girl's scrupulosity, even for those who sleep eternally in Hopkins County. Where the narrative strays from factual events and dates, my intention has been to remain faithful to the characters and to the essential drift of events as they really happened.

Making Sense of My Senses

—

I WAS BORN ON THE CREST OF A WAVE. "Prosperity is just around the corner," Hoover had assured my parents. The year was 1931, just two years before both Roosevelt and Hitler came to power. Born to parents held together by their differences, I would eventually come to understand why mine is, like so many others, a story of the human heart in conflict with itself.

I begin this story with my earliest memories of life in Arbala, Texas: memories of sight, touch, taste, smell, and sound. I am about five years old as this tale opens. At this time, Arbala still has a post office, cotton gin, blacksmith shop, general store, two churches, and a school. Arbala is in the eastern part of the state but not in the Piney Woods. It is to the north of those lush places. My family lives with my paternal grandparents, Molly and Tom Gammill. We have no money for a house of our own.

SEEING

My earliest memory is of walking out on the front porch of Grandma's and Grandpa's old house at Arbala on an early Sunday morning after a rainy May night around 1935 or 1936. The rough gray unpainted

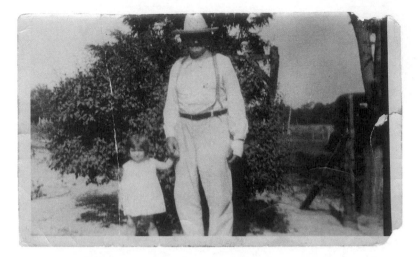

Grandpa Tom Gammill and me (Mary Lou), circa 1933.

boards of this old house and its front porch floor and the broken screen door are the backdrops for my first visual feast. I see before me a great green meadow, its boundaries stretching all the way to the blue sky. The lower parts of the meadow are filled with rainwater. Robin's egg blue wild irises, bright red Indian paintbrush, waxy yellow jonquils, and Texas bluebonnets are scattered about, fresh from Saturday night baths. I am about to explode with joy in response to this vision; at this moment, I am almost more than my body can contain.

My brother, J. T., is off to the side of the porch spinning a top, his pink cheeks as round as his fat little toes.

"I eat peanuts and sausage," he happily answers those who ask him how he got so fat.

J. T., whose initials are his actual name, has brown hair and blue eyes, which almost get lost in his round face when he grins shyly. J. T. is barefooted most of the time, winter and summer; he prefers it that way. He is dressed in striped overalls, and he is wearing a long-sleeved cotton shirt and a cap.

It is my sister, Lola Pearl, and her activity that bring my eyes back to the center of the porch. She sits on the floor surrounded by crayons and a "Big Chief" tablet. Lola Pearl has white blond hair, short and straight, with bangs straight across her forehead. Her eyes are blue and curious. Her face is intense and freckled—a serious face. She is a

Lola Pearl, J. T., and me on the farm at Arbala, circa 1935.

pretty girl. She looks like our mama, but she is more outspoken like our daddy. Lola Pearl tells me that she is making a Mother's Day card for our mama. I want to make one too, of course, but she says with all the self-importance of a nine year old, "You are too little. You will have to wait until you go to school before you can draw with crayon and make a Mother's Day card."

As I start to pout in disappointment, I notice the wildflowers that have escaped the boundaries of the meadow and are growing around the edges of the yard. I scoot down the high front steps on my bottom, walk to the flowers, and pull some of them up by the roots. With a fistful of flowers for Mama, I go back into the house looking for her. She is in the kitchen rolling out piecrusts. I hold out the flowers to her.

"Look, Mama. For you."

"Wait. I'm busy," she answers.

Finally, she wipes the flour from her hands onto her apron and the snuff that has collected at the corner of her mouth onto her hankie, and as she stoops to take the flowers from me, her soft brown hair

caresses her pretty face. Mama's features are small and regular; her eyebrows are dark and full. Her bright blue eyes have tiny flecks of yellow in them. Mama has a shy smile, not large, and a quiet, private kind of laugh. Mama is quietly pretty. She does not have long legs, but they are shapely, tapered at the ankles and full in the calves, and she wears a size six shoe. Mama is five foot two, and she weighs about one hundred pounds. She can walk under my daddy's arm when he extends it.

Mama takes a clean snuff glass from the shelf above her, dips it into the water bucket until it is about half full, and then arranges the flowers in the glass as carefully as though they were orchids in a crystal vase. Grandpa, Grandma, and Mama dip Garrett Snuff, which comes bottled in attractive fluted glasses—real glass, not plastic. These glasses are never thrown away when they are empty of snuff: they are carefully washed, placed on a shelf in the kitchen, and used for many purposes. They are our only beverage glasses, and they also serve as containers for homemade blackberry jelly.

Not to be outdone in Mother's Day gift giving, Lola Pearl soon appears in the kitchen with her colorful card, and J. T. follows with a fistful of peanuts from his overalls pocket. Mama accepts each gift as something special, but her workday goes on as usual, Mother's Day or not.

Grandpa is getting dressed for Sunday school and Mama, knowing there will be extra company today, asks him to take me along to get me out from underfoot.

Grandpa wears khaki clothing and suspenders—galluses he calls them—rather than a belt to hold up his pants. He wears a felt hat in the winter and a straw hat in the summer. Grandpa smells of liniment, and he walks with a cane. A quiet man, he is stockier and shorter than his son, my daddy.

"Get your duds on, honey. We'll go sing," he says to me. And then in his rich baritone, he raises his voice in song, "I'll fly away . . . Oh glory . . . I'll fly away. . . ."

I jump up and down in affirmation and anticipation. We polish my Sunday shoes, black patent Roman sandals, with a leftover buttermilk biscuit. The biscuit contains lard and makes the shoes shine. I pull on my Sunday dress, the one Mama made for me from the pretty

print fabric of a large cotton flour sack. Mama smooths my short, straight hair, and I am ready to go.

Grandpa is the churchgoer in the family. He is unusual in our family in that he seems to recognize his wife as an equal partner. Except, of course, he is a little more equal on Sundays since he has time to go to Sunday school at the Arbala Methodist Church while she stays home and cooks for him, the preacher, and other hungry Sunday schoolers who might be in need of a good meal.

My daddy does not go to church on Sunday or any other day. He plays dominoes or throws horseshoes with the other young men outside the general store in Arbala. Sometimes they buy cheese and crackers and sit on the steps of the store to eat them. My daddy is a big man. He is six foot two and weighs about two hundred pounds, but he is not fat. He is rawboned, energetic, and restless. He has a brown face and hands from constant exposure to the sun. His long-sleeved shirts always cover his arms except when he rolls up the sleeves. His striped overalls cover the rest of his body. His work shoes are big and heavy. He calls them brogans. Daddy wears straw hats in the summer and always when he works in the fields. He wears his best felt Stetson hat when he goes to town and his second best Stetson hat when he is working outside in the winter. His torso and legs, untouched by the sun, are surprisingly white, almost a milk white. He has blue eyes in a leathery face and dark brown hair, soft textured like mine. Daddy has a straight, longish nose and large ears that stand out slightly from his head, but he is altogether a handsome man in a rugged sort of way.

My daddy does not dip snuff. He smokes cigarettes that he rolls himself by using items extracted from his shirt pocket: a package of thin cigarette papers and smoking tobacco contained in a flat, red can of Prince Albert with a flip-open top or a little white cotton sack of Bull Durham with a drawstring top. Carefully creasing the center of the paper with the forefinger of his right hand and cupping the two edges of the paper with his thumb and second finger, he makes a little groove to hold the tobacco. In his left hand he holds the Prince Albert or Bull Durham containers and carefully pours exactly the right amount of tobacco into the paper receptacle. This done, he returns the container of tobacco and the unused papers to his shirt pocket and uses the fingers of both hands to roll the cigarette into a perfect elon-

gation, leaving a small margin of paper at the top that he licks and then folds over the cigarette to hold it together. I am fascinated with this ritual. When I grow up, I will smoke cigarettes.

Today Grandpa takes me by the hand, and we walk the muddy mile to Sunday school. There, in the Arbala Methodist Church I see a vision of human loveliness that comes close to the vision of nature's loveliness I had witnessed earlier that morning from the front porch of the old house. A teenage girl plays the organ; she is tall and slender and is wearing a purple velvet dress and bright red lipstick. Her dark luxurious hair falls about her shoulders. She has bewitching red fingernails, and I am mesmerized by her bright beauty.

TOUCH

Until I first touch Ponzell's wonderfully curly hair, I think all human hair is like mine, soft and feathery and likely to get tangled. Ponzell has come this Christmas morning to Arbala with Aunt Settie, his mother, from Birch Creek Bottom, a nearby black settlement. The grown-ups call it "nigger town." At this time in my life, I assume that this is the name for all black people, but I can plainly see that this is not a town at all, just a few houses clustered around a bottom near the creek.

From Arbala, Birch Creek Bottom is about one third of the way to the nearby town of Sulphur Springs. The houses here are unpainted, or else the paint is peeling, like that on our own house. Sometimes they are simply whitewashed rather than painted. Most of the houses rest on blocks, like ours, but these seem to cling closer to the road. These owners, usually having less acreage than the people in Arbala, have to use the land at the back of the house for planting small crops. Almost every house has collard greens, a food staple, growing in the side yards. Every household has a hog pen down the hill, sloping toward the creek that often overflows. Dogs, chickens, pigs, and big, bony cows meander around the premises. At our house, Grandma and Grandpa let the dogs and chickens have the run of the yards, but Grandma will not allow the pigpen to be near the house. Grandma and Grandpa have a rocker or two on the front porch but not other old furniture, which you might see on a Birch Creek Bottom front porch. Just like in Arbala, an old gentleman is certain to be sitting on the

porch here, visiting with all who pass by. Certainly someone he can visit with will be walking about here in Birch Creek Bottom. In Arbala, more people pass by in wagons and cars and seem to have time only to wave. The women in Birch Creek Bottom tie their hair in colorful rags rather than cover their heads with poke bonnets as the women of Arbala do. Their small frame church is within convenient walking distance of everyone in the settlement, and their funerals are much bigger events and have far greater church member participation than the funerals at Arbala. As in our own house at Arbala, every house here has the barest essentials in the way of furniture: iron bedsteads with rusty springs, a wood-burning cookstove and heating stove or maybe a fireplace, coal oil lamps, an eating table, and a few straight-backed wooden chairs. No one has indoor plumbing or electricity, of course.

Ponzell and Aunt Settie have walked up the road to our house in Arbala this morning to help with all the extra work brought by the extra company, probably about twenty to thirty kinfolk. I am not allowed to go to church with Grandpa today because I have torn my Sunday dress and Mama has not had time to mend it.

While Grandpa, uncles, cousins, J. T., and Lola Pearl are at church, and while aunts are putting last minute touches on dishes they brought, Aunt Settie helps Grandma and Mama in the kitchen. Aunt Settie is round as a beanbag, and I slip a chocolate-covered cherry, a rare Christmas treat at our house, into her apron pocket as she works. Warm from her labors at the woodstove, she forgets about it there, and it melts.

"Lord a mercy, chile, our candy done melt," she calls out to me.

I expect to be soundly scolded as she gazes at the brown goo. Instead, she laughs uproariously as if I have made the best joke of the day. She hugs me, and I am lost in the folds of her enormity. How I love her at that moment.

It is Ponzell's job to pick up trash and sweep the bare dirt yards, and I follow him outside. Ponzell is as tall and slender as his mother is round. They are both a rich milk chocolate color. I beg Ponzell to "make me fly."

"Young un," he says to me, "stop pesterin' me and wait 'til I get this here yard swept."

And then, "Fly," he shouts, as he lifts me over his head, and I flap

my arms and legs wildly. To steady myself, I put my hand on the top of his head and grasp a handful of his hair. I have often touched my own hair, of course. I know the feel of the hair of everyone in my family, but I have never touched hair like this before. From time to time, for the rest of the day, I touch my own hair. When Ponzell lifts me in play, I shyly reach out and pat his head, thrilling to the bounce and life I feel there.

TASTE

Black Draught is a dark, strong-tasting, vile-smelling, liquid medicine used as a cure-all for every childhood ailment in our family. I cannot swallow it without holding my nose as Mama forces the spoonful into my mouth. And it is not as if swallowing it ends the matter—the taste lingers long afterward, much like that of castor oil, another childhood cure-all. Although everyone keeps telling me castor oil has no taste, I cannot be fooled. That oily feeling it leaves in my mouth is to me among the worst of all tastes. I never see an adult ingest either medicine.

Of course, I remember flavors other than medicinal; for example, dewberry shortcake comes to mind. In early spring, this twin of the blackberry grows wild along the fencerows and in the woods of East Texas. Its berries are fat, sweet, and juicy. In dewberry season, we come back to the house after a berry-picking expedition, our arms and legs covered with scratches from the thorns of the berry vines and angry red bites from the chiggers that hide there.

A ritual follows: wash the berries very carefully, for they spill their juice easily; put them in a large bowl; mash them like potatoes; add sugar; then let the mixture stand while the sugar soaks into it and Mama bakes the piecrust. As soon as the extra-crispy crusts are cool, place a layer of crust in a deep dish. On top of that goes a cup of the berry mixture, and then the whole process is repeated until all of the crusts and all of the berries are used. After the shortcake is spooned into bowls, we pass around a pitcher of thick, fresh cream skimmed off that morning's milk to pour over the top of each serving.

"Scrumptious!," we say in between little moans of pleasure.

We wait all week for the tastes of Sunday: platters of fried chicken, bowls of cream gravy, mashed potatoes, fried okra, biscuits by the

dozens, chocolate pie, and coconut cake. Chickens, of course, must first be chased down, captured, beheaded, dunked in scalding water, plucked, eviscerated, washed, and battered before they can be fried. Potatoes have to be dug and okra gathered from the garden. The gravy, biscuits, pies, and cakes are miracles Mama and Grandma create from large sacks of flour and sugar and buckets of lard bought at the general store and hauled home in the wagon. The eggs come from our squawking chickens and the butter is made in our churn from the rich milk of our best Jersey cow, Old Crip. Best of all, though, is boiled custard, a beverage we have only at Christmastime. (Its closest counterpart today is grocery store eggnog.) Grandma saves sugar, fresh eggs from the Rhode Island Red hens that roam freely in the yards, and cream skimmed from Old Crip's milk. Finally, when the big day comes and the boiled custard is cooked to perfection, Grandma pours it into a big glass bowl and sets it out on the back porch to cool. I play outside, but I keep my eye on the custard bowl.

"What's that you poured into Grandma's boiled custard?" I ask my Uncle Live whose real name is A. Lively Day.

"It's just something that will make it taste better. Don't tell Grandma," he warns me.

I don't believe him. Nothing on earth could make Grandma's boiled custard any better than it already is. Pretty soon my daddy walks out on the porch, reaches into his hip pocket, pulls out a bottle, and he, too, adds a stream of liquid to the boiled custard.

My Aunt Clara, who is married to A. Lively Day, and who is walking around the house to come in the back door with a roasting pan, sees what my daddy is doing and yells to her mother inside the house, "Oh, Molly, oh, Molly, come out here and get this boiled custard before these men ruin it with their whiskey."

On Christmas, as on an ordinary Sunday, the men eat at first table with the preacher. While the women walk back and forth serving the men, I stand behind the door that leads into the kitchen, my mouth watering and stomach pinching, peeking around to see if there will be any food left for me. I am too big now to nurse, and besides, I can still hear Aunt Clara, Daddy's youngest sister and the baby of their family, shaming me when I was even smaller and had tried to pull Mama behind the door with me so I could nurse.

"Uh, huh," she had begun in her whiney put-on voice, the one she

reserved for teasing little kids, "Tryin' to get a little titty are you? Aren't you ashamed? A big girl like you, lookin' for a little titty."

No one thinks to question why the men should always eat at first table, or why the women should stand ready to refill the empty dishes and freshen the drinks, or why the children had to wait until second table. The men in our extended family have certain privileges, and that is that. One privilege they enjoy is to go off together in a little group after a big meal while the women and children eat and clean up the kitchen. One day after just such a meal, Grandma betrays her lack of satisfaction with this status quo. Grandma, who builds her own cooking and washing fires with no help from the men, is struggling with something heavy in the kitchen.

"Where are the men? They're never around anywhere when I need one of them to lift something for me," she says to no one in particular.

"They're off smoking cigarettes and telling lies," I say, mimicking what I have heard an aunt say earlier that day about the men. For many years, among the female members of the extended Gammill family, "Off smoking cigarettes and telling lies" was the abbreviated punch line answer to the query, "Where are the men?"

Food and religion are inextricably bound in my child's mind. When the preacher drones on and on with the blessing at mealtime, my prayer is always simple and to the point, "Lord, make them save something for me."

To break the monotony of one hot July afternoon, my cousins, sister, brother, and I, the youngest of the lot, join together to hold a pretend church service. Each person is to take a turn preaching the sermon, standing on a tree stump facing an old bench where the "members of the congregation" sit. Grandpa is seated among the listeners. All the other "preachers" deliver their sermons with great seriousness, and then it is my turn, at last. I climb up on the stump, face the "congregation," wag my finger at them, and begin, "Brothers and Sisters, the Lord said, 'Don't eat no more cabbage and potatoes for so long as ye may live.'"

The big kids all laugh at me; a couple of the boys even roll around in the dirt yard, collapsed in laughter, but Grandpa takes me on his lap and hugs me.

Easier going, more gentle, and softer than my daddy, Grandpa has

a more restful temperament than his son. He can sit and rock and rest. Grandpa never loses his temper and cusses like my daddy.

SMELL

Yeast bread baking in the oven, honey just robbed from the beehives, freshly plowed earth, the outhouse, coal oil lamps, stinkbugs, and Miss Dodie's perfume are the smells of my childhood.

Although we bake and eat cornbread or buttermilk biscuits with every meal, we never have yeast rolls (the bread that makes me mad with desire when I smell it baking in the oven) unless my Aunt Lola comes from her teaching job in West Texas to visit us. At her elbow as she mixes the ingredients and then places the dough in a bowl to rise, I am never far from the kitchen, and my anticipation rises with the dough as the morning wears on. When the bread is placed in the oven, I am ecstatic. The yeast bread is delicious to eat, but it is even more delightful to smell as it bakes in the oven of the big, black woodstove, and the aroma wafts through the kitchen where I wait.

Each of us kids has been stung by bees so we know to stay away from the beehives in the pasture on the day Daddy robs them. He pulls on a hat with something like a face veil attached and fills a bellows with smoke. He wears extra clothing, long gloves, and a serious face. Grandpa goes with him to the hives. Just once I get close enough to watch. Daddy pumps the bellows, the smoke invades the hives, and the bees fly out. Crazily they fly about while he reaches in and extracts the honeycombs. Some bees try to get back into the hive, and Daddy's arms are covered with the buzzing creatures. I am afraid for him. The scents of fear, smoke, heat, clover, and flowers blend and invade my sense of smell. Soon we are back at the house and looking at our treasure. I ask for a piece of the honeycomb. All my senses are at full throttle as I chew this morsel.

At the very end of winter, my daddy hitches the horse to the turning plow and breaks ground for the year's first crop. With the reins looped loosely over his muscular shoulders and his rough brown hands gripping the plow handles, Daddy turns over the old earth and exposes the new, just below. I love to follow barefoot in the freshly plowed rows behind my daddy, digging my toes into the cool earth. The smells of the just-awakened earth and of the old growth going

under, of the new growth all around, and of the buds about to burst teach me all I need to know about renewal.

The Safest Place in the World to Sit is in my daddy's lap. He feels warm, and though he always works hard and perspires freely, I never notice body odor. Daddy smokes cigarettes, but he never smells like stale tobacco smoke. He just smells like Daddy and no one else, and it is a good smell. Daddy bathes every day, which is not easy to do with no indoor plumbing or bathing facilities easily available, and if he is getting ready to go to town, rather than to the field, he takes special care. Mama starches and presses his khaki clothing until the creases of his trousers are razor sharp and his shirts are crisp. This clothing is for town or other special wear, but even his everyday clothing, Mama irons carefully. For town trips, he prefers to wear his polished cowboy boots.

Mama never wears store-bought fragrances, but like Daddy, she always smells clean, like her homemade soap and our dried-outside-in-the-fresh-air clothing.

Daddy never cuts his own hair or ours. He says he does not want us to look as though we have had bowls turned over our heads while our hair was trimmed around the edges. He and my brother go to the barbershop in town, and later, when he is making a little money, Daddy gets a barbershop shave and haircut and a shoeshine from the black man who works in the back of the barbershop. More often, Daddy shaves himself at home while in his undershirt and cotton briefs. He uses a straight-edged razor that he sharpens on a leather strop hanging near the mirror above the stand that supports a basin of water. He swishes his shaving brush into a mug, which contains soap and water, and lathers generously before he pulls the straight razor in short, downward movements across his face. In later years, he uses a safety razor. Much to my disappointment, he does not use the famous Burma-Shave cream that had been made a household word by jingles on numerous highway billboards. If Daddy has some aftershave on hand, he splashes that on his face with a slight slapping motion and then rubs his face against mine so I can feel the cool smoothness and smell the freshness of his face.

Breakfast smells are special. When Daddy is home, he always helps Mama cook breakfast. His specialties are hotcakes, which he calls flapjacks, served with Mama's homemade butter and sorghum

syrup he made himself and his home-cured fried ham, which he serves with red-eye gravy and Mama's flaky biscuits. Although I would never say Daddy was Mama's equal as a cook, his presence in the kitchen always made breakfast taste better.

The outhouse always smells of lime, weathered boards, and the soft, sometimes rain-dampened pages of the Sears Roebuck catalog, which serve the dual role of both toilet paper and picture book. All the pages are soft; most are sepia tinted; none are glossy. The bed I share with my sister and the flannel nightgowns we wear often smell like pee in the mornings when we awake, because she sometimes cannot rouse herself to use the slop jar under the bed when she needs to relieve herself during the night. Coal oil lamps give us our only light at night, and the acrid aroma of a kerosene-soaked wick is with me yet. Though stinkbugs emit an odor familiar to many, the smell of Miss Dodie's perfume is one that only a select few have known.

After having lived in Dallas for many years, Miss Dodie came to live with her mother on the farm next to ours after her divorce. We are all envious that she has a car, money, and the freedom to come and go as she pleases. Miss Dodie also loves to wear perfume. When she drives down the dry, dirt road, causing dust to fly in our faces while we are stooping over the brittle cotton stalks pulling the white fluffy fiber from its bolls, we joke that we cannot see Miss Dodie, but we sure can smell her.

HEARING

"It's ready," Mama says, after testing the clabbered milk in the churn to see if it is the right consistency and temperature to make butter. She sits close in front of the butter churn, her knees together and slightly to the side. Slosh, slish, slosh, slish goes the churn dash, up and down into the milk below.

"I want to churn. I want to churn," I beg.

Sometimes Mama lets me attempt a few down and up movements of the churn dash. When I do succeed in bringing the dash all the way down or all the way up, the milk sloshes up through the opening in the lid and splashes on us.

"Ring. Ring. Ring. R - i - n - g." Three shorts and a long.

I want to climb up on a chair to reach the telephone on the wall,

raise the earpiece to my ear, and speak into the mouthpiece, but I know I am not allowed to do that, even though three shorts and a long *is* the signal that the call is for us. I notice that Grandma will sometimes pick up the earpiece and listen without speaking even when the rings are not three shorts and a long.

Another sound that I can still hear is that of Daddy cussing at the cows when they break out of the pasture. Daddy cussing at anything that goes wrong is a childhood sound permanently embedded in my head. I recall Daddy cussing, sometimes just to be cussing, and Mama responding in disapproval, "Tice!"

Daddy singing "Poor Babes in the Woods" to me as he cuddles me in his lap is another unforgettable sound:

> Poor babes in the woods, poor babes in the woods.
> They were stolen away on a bright summer's day.
> And they cried and they cried
> And they cried 'til they died.
> Poor babes in the woods, poor babes in the woods.
> And the robins so red did over them spread
> Strawberry leaves to cover their heads.
> Poor babes in the woods, poor babes in the woods.

Although the words and the deep, mournful way he sings them always make me cry, I never quit loving that little song.

And before I grow too heavy to lift into the air, I sit astride his foot when he is in a chair with his legs crossed and beg him to sing, "His Name Was Dapple Gray":

> I had a little horsey—his name was Dapple Gray,
> His legs were made of cornstalks, his body made of hay,
> I bridled him, I saddled him, I rode him into town,
> Along came a whirlwind and blew him upside down.

While singing the first three lines, he bounces me up and down with his foot. When he reaches the fourth line, he tosses me into his lap and turns me upside down.

Thus it went for the first six years of my life when my little world was new, and I wore my senses like nerve endings. From the first awareness of sound and touch to my earliest memories of color, taste, and smell—all are closely interwoven with family interaction.

End of the Beginning

IT IS NOW THE WINTER OF 1937, and my family is about to turn a corner, still without much expectation of the prosperity Hoover had promised was on its way some six years earlier.

Daddy has always hoped he could have his own place some day. He has been paying a few dollars a month for a couple of years on some land across the creek in another community. The old house on that land is unlivable, or so Daddy thinks, and so we have stayed on at Grandpa's, hoping we could save enough money to build a house on our own land. Grandpa is a good, loving man, law-abiding and willing to turn the other cheek. But he is not ambitious, and Daddy realizes he will have to get out on his own in order to support us.

In true *Grapes of Wrath* tradition, my grandparents, even with my parents pitching in to help, can no longer keep up the mortgage payments on their farm. With compound interest, they are steadily losing ground, and the bank is about to foreclose. When the notice of foreclosure comes, Daddy tries desperately to raise the money to save his parents' farm, but he is already committed to buying our own place and fails to raise the necessary funds to save the old home place—a regret he will feel for the rest of his life.

Grandma and Grandpa move to a little rent house near the general

store in Arbala and settle into retirement with their meager "old age pensions." This is probably the first time they have been alone since the birth of their first child so many years before. In a few weeks, however, they take in two motherless grandsons to raise. Grandpa is no longer able to do hard work in the fields, but he is a big help to Grandma as she works around the house. He shells peas for canning, picks turnip greens and then washes them free of sand and little bugs so Grandma can cook them for dinner, gathers eggs, milks the cow, and mends things that need to be fixed. Of course, Grandma is as busy as ever now that she once again has young children to care for.

My family moves about three miles away to the old dilapidated house Daddy had thought unlivable, to the land he has been making payments on, up the hilly, slippery-when-wet, clay road across the creek from Arbala. The new community we are moving to is called Seymore, but it is not on any map or road sign. Daddy explains that since Seymore does not have a post office, it has no official name. He says that if someone asks why we are moving so far away, we should explain that we are moving not to the official Seymore located way out in West Texas, but just a few miles away to the little Seymore, named for its first settlers.

On Our Own

IT IS A SNOWY FEBRUARY DAY; the first snow I have ever seen. J. T., Lola Pearl, and Mama herd the cows ahead of the wagon that holds all of our belongings, Daddy, and me. We are on our way to a new community and life on our own. An ice storm during the previous night has left bony fingers hanging from branches of the bois d'arc trees down by the creek. The frozen fields stretch away into the distance to the point where, just on the other side of the woods along the creek bank, the bleak hills rise silently, flushed with red in the morning sun. Finally we arrive at our new home. The branches of the big oak in the front yard make a delicate tracing of white against the dark barn. Little rickrack icicles glisten on the barbed wire fences. The white, wintery world sings to me.

Daddy tries to clean bird nests out of the fireplace chimney and cuts wood for a fire. Heat from the fireplace is all the warmth we will have for the whole house. And for now, it is the only place Mama has to cook. Daddy tells Mama not to worry that there is no cookstove. He knows where he can get one for five dollars. Mama notices right away that the house has no window screens. He tells her he will have them made and hung before summer. Mama arranges our belongings in the cold house. We do not have much in the way of cooking utensils or

furniture. We did not need much except our beds when we lived with Grandma and Grandpa at Arbala. They gave us everything they did not need for the rental house they moved to, and so we have enough to begin housekeeping.

The next morning, I play outside in the snow and suck on icicles hanging from the clothesline and the tree branches while Lola Pearl and J. T. go off to school. I think I will never be old enough to go to school. Someday, Mama tells me, I can go with them just to visit. Seymore has a two-room school—with a "big" room and a "little" room—and two teachers. The designations of big and little have more to do with the age and size of the students than with the dimensions of the rooms, which are about the same size.

That afternoon, Mama scoops up some of the clean snow, puts it into a bowl, adds a little sugar and vanilla, and we have ice cream. Better than scrumptious! Around 4:00 P.M., Daddy bundles me up and takes me along for a ride in the wagon when he goes to pick up Lola Pearl and J. T. after school dismisses. The experience is almost as good as being a pupil, I think. I love being alone with my daddy and having *all* of his attention and not having to share it with my older and bigger and smarter sister and brother.

Seymore also has a small general store and a blacksmith shop. The blacksmith shop is fascinating with its deep, dark interior and roaring fire. The smith has more power than the devil himself as he dips the metal into the fire, holds it with his tongs until it turns a bright red, then places it on the anvil. Clang, clang goes the hammer. Sparks fly. It is better than the Fourth of July or fireworks at Christmas. The smith is a very important person because farmers still plow with horses. The horses have to be shod and the plows sharpened. This particular smithy has devised an improvement to a standard plow and so is given some regard in the community.

The Baptist Church members meet in the big room of the school for their Sunday services. The Church of Christ members have their own small church, and if there are people of other religious persuasions in Seymore, they must travel to surrounding communities for their church services.

I receive a "play pretty"—a little tin tea set made in China or Japan for Christmas the winter we move. I play with it every day, inviting imaginary friends to join me while my brother and sister are at

school. But I can only sip tea for so long, and since that is the only bought toy I have, I am always in search of adventure outside the house. One day, during one of Daddy's long absences (he seems to be gone from home now for longer and longer stretches of time), my grandpa walks over from Arbala to help Mama mend one of the fences where the cows have broken through to graze in the neighbor's pasture. I follow the grown-ups, of course. After the fence is mended, Grandpa hands me the hammer to take back to the house and leaves on foot, as he had come, for Arbala. Mama has already returned to the house and other chores, so I am left alone with the hammer. As I walk toward the house, I start to toss it in the air, intending to catch it before it lands on my toes. Gradually I become bolder, and the hammer flies higher. The last toss sails high overhead. I cannot get my hands in position in time to catch it on its return, and the claw end of the hammer digs into my scalp.

The blow stuns me but does not knock me unconscious. In an instant, I feel the warm, sticky blood trickle down my face. I know I will be scolded and maybe spanked for playing with the hammer when I have been told to take it to the house and put it away, but that fear pales in comparison to the fear of the blood I taste. I know I am in big trouble, so with head throbbing and blood spurting, I run for Mama to fix it. Faced with a bleeding child, no telephone, no car, no doctor, no husband, and no other grown-up there to help her, she takes me in her arms and runs to the nearest neighbor, a half-mile down the dirt road. Aunt Cubby, the matriarch of the extended family living there, knows what to do. She reaches into the chimney of the wood-burning fireplace, where all winter the soot has been collecting, grabs a handful of the black residue, and packs it into the gaping wound on the top of my head. The bleeding stops. I am put to bed, and all I remember of the aftereffects is the blood-saturated, sticky, smelly, stiff-as-a-board hair that cannot be washed for a week or more.

I cannot say the whole experience was bleak though; it was at this time that I learned illness brings special compensations. For once, I was the center of attention, and I opened my pores to receive it.

Finally the day comes when I can visit school. Mama has made me a simple dress from a flower-printed flour sack, has cleaned and polished my shoes, and scrubbed me in the rainwater that has been warming in the tin tub. I feel like a fairy princess on her way to the ball

as I stand waiting that morning to be off on the walk to school. I can still hear my brother and sister arguing about which one will take me to school as his or her guest. Neither of them wants me. Lola Pearl says I belong in the little room with my brother, and J. T. says that everyone will laugh at him if he comes to school with a girl and that I should go with my sister to the big room. The argument escalates to tears, screaming, and pushing, and still I hold firm: this is the day I *am* going to school. Somebody is going to take me—Mama promised. I do not remember how it was settled; probably I visited in both rooms that day, but it is the little room that I remember.

Mary Helen, a first grader with large, soft gray eyes, moves over at her little desk so I can sit with her. I already know the name of and all about the teacher in the little room, I think, but her beauty surprises me. A town girl, she has been protected from the sun, never having had to work in the fields as my own mother and most of the women I know have. Her skin is flawless, her hair is the softest brown, her eyes are a beautiful shade of gray, and her laugh is soft and bubbly. All the pupils call her what sounds like "MissAhMay." When I am older and a real pupil who can read, I learn her name is Miss Annie Mae Whisenant.

I am aware of the embarrassment my presence in the little room is causing my brother, so I try to keep my distance from him. This is not a deliberate act on my part to save him embarrassment—it is an effort to save my body from a few bruises.

This is the day I fall in love with books. My sister remembers that we had some Zane Gray books Daddy traded for when we lived at Arbala. She says she remembers lying in bed at night, pressing her ear to the wall, and listening to Mama read to Daddy and Grandma as they sat by the fireplace in the front room. I cannot remember books in our house at all until my sister and brother bring home their schoolbooks. The day I visit the little room, the colorful books I see make me salivate. Just think, next year I will be a *real* pupil, not a guest, and I will have my very own book.

HOG-KILLING DAY

Our second winter in Seymore, Daddy butchered a hog he had been fattening for months. We fed that hog every scrap of table food left over from our meals, even the dishwater, which contained grease and

fragments of food. We children had to take turns slopping the hog. Sometimes we fed him dried corn on the cob or a mash Daddy made by mixing ground grain he bought at the feed store with hot water to make a sort of cereal treat for the hog. Mr. Porker grew very fat, just what Daddy wanted. He always insisted that the fat be left on his meat when it was cooked. "It's not fit to eat without the tallow," he often said.

That second winter at Seymore was not as cold as our first one, and it seemed that the weather would never be cold enough to do the butchering, which had to take place out-of-doors. Finally, late one afternoon, a norther blew in, and Daddy knew the time was right. He went to see three of the neighbor men to ask for help in butchering the next morning.

At dawn, the neighbors are at our house, ready to help. Daddy already has fires burning under two large iron wash pots filled with water. The men all go to work building a scaffolding from which the hog carcass will hang. Each kid is assigned a job. Mine is to help my sister feed the fires with wood. Bundled to the eyeballs against the cold wind, I pitch in and do my best work at butchering time. It is not that I relish the death part of it—I have to cover my eyes and ears when the actual slaughter takes place—but I love the excitement generated by so many people working so quickly in the cold and by the thought of the good ham and bacon to come. I know that this hog will be the only meat we have all year, except for chickens, which do not count because we eat a chicken every Sunday. Besides, I have not liked the taste of chicken ever since the day a baby chick got under my foot as I stomped out of the house in a tantrum and smashed the poor little creature.

After the men kill and bleed the hog, they dip him several times into the scalding water and then hang him from the scaffolding by two feet. With sharp knives, they scrape the hair and hide from the animal and then slit him down the center from top to bottom to disembowel him. All the innards are placed in dishpans, and the carcass is left hanging for awhile to become even colder before it is cut up. We kids have to stand guard to keep the excited dogs away.

Precious little of the hog goes to waste. All the helpers go home with a day's supply of the fresh meat. Since none of us have ice, we find inventive ways to preserve the meat. My Grandma Gammill at Arbala gets the hog's head. She is the one who knows how to make souse. Our black neighbors down in Birch Creek Bottom, who have

even less than we, get the entrails from which they will make chitlins. Another family, who had once lived in the north, knows how to pickle pig's feet, and so the feet are theirs. A certain amount of the fat has been set aside for making sausage; a certain amount is packed in salt for those lean days when we have no meat other than this "fat back" with which to season the vegetables, or slice, roll in cornmeal, and fry for breakfast; and a certain amount—actually, all that is left over— is tossed aside in a large dishpan to be rendered into lard and home-made soap.

Daddy's specialty is making sausage and smoking hams. Into a big dishpan or small washtub, Daddy grinds the pork. He adds plenty of sage, lots of dried red pepper, and a special sausage seasoning he buys at the store. He uses choice parts of the hog for the sausage, making certain he has just the right amount of fat, and he mixes it all thoroughly. Daddy always says the secret of good sausage is in the mixing. Mama has made sausage casings—little round, elongated white cotton sacks with drawstrings at the tops—out of empty sugar sacks, and when Daddy is satisfied that the sausage is mixed to perfection, Mama takes over, packing the sausage mixture into the little casings she has made ahead of time. Daddy then hangs the sacks of sausage from the rafters on the back porch or in the smokehouse. There the sausages will dry, and there they will remain until we need them.

Daddy cures the hams and shoulders by rubbing a sugar, smoke, and curing mixture into them and hanging them to dry in a shed we call a smokehouse, although we never actually have a fire going there. Mama cooks and cans some of the meat in glass jars after we have had our fill of the fresh pork. The only other fresh meat we are likely to have this year will depend upon whether or not we have twenty-five cents to spare when a neighbor kills a cow and sells the fresh beef. Even then, we can buy enough for only one meal because we have no ice. I never fail to get sick from having eaten too much boiled back-bone on hog-butchering day.

THE WASH POT

Every country family had a big wash pot—sometimes, two or three. The pot was always made of cast iron and always black. It was Mama's job to render lard from the leftover fat meat after butchering, and that

is where the big, black pot came in. First, she would get a good, strong wood fire going outdoors under the wash pot. Then she would toss chunks of fat into the pot and stir the bubbly grease with a long wooden spoon until all the fat liquefied. Once cooled and solidified, this became the lard she used for cooking. In the days before peanut, safflower, or corn oil, lard was a must-have in every kitchen. Perhaps it did clog more than a few arteries; it also helped make piecrusts to die for.

Later, the pot would be used to make lye soap. To make it, lye was stirred into the hot fat. Eventually, it would solidify, and Mama would cut it into bars of soap. I know that homemade lye was sometimes also made from oak wood ash, but the lye we used came in a can from the store.

The pot's most frequent use came on wash day. Even in winter, the wash pot was filled with water and shavings from the lye soap and set over an outdoor fire to boil. Into the pot went all the dirty clothes, which Mama poked deep into the water from time to time with a broom handle. After the clothes were in the hot water long enough, Mama lifted them out of the pot with the same broom handle and into one of two number three tubs waiting on a plank supported by sawhorses. One tub she used for scrubbing any still-soiled clothing on a scrub board until she was satisfied it was spotless. She then transferred it to the other tub filled with rinse water. I was often called on to do the rinsing as I grew older. Mama called it "rinching" as her grandmother had. I was not good at hand wringing the wash before it could be hung on the clothesline to dry, so Mama would take it from me and do it herself. I soon learned that I could get out of almost anything I hated to do simply by outwaiting her. Any water that was left in the pot on wash day, Mama took into the house and poured onto the wooden floors, sweeping it around and out. This cleansing made the whole house smell wonderfully fresh.

At Christmas, this same pot was used to boil the hams from the smokehouse; at school closings, it held Hopkins County Stew; and at fish fries by creekside, it held golden brown catfish fillets bubbling in grease.

For more than a year, we felt fortunate to have our own place, enough food, and good health. Daddy had been clearing the land and selling some of the wood he had cut, but he never got around to buy-

ing those window screens he had promised to Mama on the first day we moved to Seymore and set up housekeeping on our own. Now, there was no money to buy screens. Daddy found some old ones and hung those, but they were rusty and full of holes. In the summer, we had to raise the windows to get a breeze. When the windows were open, the flies swarmed in. We sprayed and hung fly-catcher strips that looked like yellow daisies. We swatted and shooed those flies, but nothing discouraged them at mealtime. We took turns trying to keep the flies away from the table and the food by fanning the air near those who were eating. At first, the flies seemed only a giant nuisance. Later, when sickness struck at our house, the flies seemed to be the culprits—likely carriers of a deadly germ.

TYPHOID FEVER

In the summer of 1938, my sister woke one morning with a raging fever. None of the usual home remedies would bring her fever down. She became delirious, so Daddy brought a doctor from Sulphur Springs out to the farm to examine her. He diagnosed typhoid fever and said that he would have to send a sample of our well water off to Austin, Texas, to be tested. Until the safety of the water was determined, we were to drink no more water from the well. We hauled water to drink and to cook with from my aunt's house in town. J. T. and I were examined, given some sort of inoculations, and taken away from the house to stay with kinfolk. On the day we left home to stay with relatives, Mama came down with the fever. Everyone was afraid they both would die. I felt the anxiety in my bones and had bad dreams about falling through space, only to be abruptly awakened as I caught myself in midfall.

The tests on the water samples showed that, yes, the typhoid germ was in our water. Then someone remembered that years before we moved here, in the exact spot our water well now stood, another family had lost two children to the fever. The doctor speculated that that family had not disposed of its bodily waste carefully—not far enough away from the water source—so the germ lived on. This was what the doctor suspected, but Mama always thought it was the pesky flies who brought the typhoid germ.

Although I worried about Mama and my sister, I enjoyed the

forced vacation away from home because I got to be with my favorite girl cousin and away from my teasing brother, who was staying with another relative. Daddy hired a woman from a neighboring community to take care of our sick ones and to keep house. She came to live with us, and we were soon allowed to come home because there would now be someone in the house to look after J. T. and me.

Her name was Alfie May Knight, and more than anything else, I remember the way she curled her hair. Mama never curled our hair or her own, nor did she go to the beauty shop. When home permanents became popular, we gave those to each other, but that was much later. With her hair still damp after shampooing, Alfie May would roll a strand of hair over a lead pencil then slip the pencil out with her right hand while holding the curl in place with her left hand. Next, she would open a bobby pin with her teeth and insert one end of it into the center of the roll of hair to hold it in place. When her hair dried, she removed the bobby pins, but she did not brush through her hair. I stood behind her from beginning to end as she performed this ritual, and I can still see the two horizontal rows of Vienna sausage curls resting on the back of her head near her neckline, but I cannot remember what her "do" looked like from the front. I also remember being excited about the possibility of introducing Alfie May to my Aunt Clara. Although I was too shy to actually do it, I would imagine saying, "Mrs. Knight, meet Mrs. Day."

Finally, both my mother and sister recovered from the typhoid fever. My sister had lost all of her hair, but it came back curly. I began to covet her blond curls beyond measure when, more than once, I heard my own hair described as "straight as a board" or "straight as a poker." I had already begun to think of myself as ugly when one day around this time a boy schoolmate said to me, "Did you pour black shoe polish on your head?" I was so humiliated I wanted to die. Recalling that incident, I realize that my hair must have been bright and shiny, something to have been envied rather than ashamed of. But that is not the way I saw it then. Typhoid fever seemed to me a small price to pay for curly blond hair.

Miraculously, Mama did not lose her hair with the fever. She wore her long brown hair loose only when she had been a very young woman, before children and hard work; when she sat resting to let her hair dry after she had shampooed it; or when she slept. The rest

of the time, she wound it into a ball or bun shape and then anchored it to the back of her head with hairpins. Several times she had her hair cut short at the barbershop that Daddy frequented in Sulphur Springs, but she would not let the barber shingle it in the back when that style was popular for women because she thought a shingle looked too harsh.

I remember Mama letting me comb her hair once as she sat for a few minutes on the front porch to rest just after the sun had gone down. I got carried away, as I was prone to do, and started to twist her hair around the comb. I thought I was curling it, but eventually I had the comb so entangled in her hair I could not remove it. I do not know how she finally got the comb disentangled. I do know that it was the first time she ever got mad at me—maybe the only time she ever got that mad at me—and I felt simply awful about causing her all that discomfort.

BARTERING

Mama and Lola Pearl had remained at home throughout their illnesses, so there were no hospital bills, but there were many doctor, medicine, and caretaker bills to pay. Daddy doubled his efforts that fall and winter after the typhoid to pay those debts. He turned to syrup making because syrup was a good bartering tool. The people to whom we owed money agreed to accept the syrup and cordwood as payment for the debts.

Syrup making, which belongs almost exclusively to factories now, was once the job of small farmers—a joint undertaking. Cutting and hauling the cane to the mill was no job for children or weaklings. Daddy cut much of it himself and traded work with other farmers to cut the remainder. Once at the mill, owned by another farmer, the most careful of the workers fed the cane into the press, which was powered by a mule. Harnessed to the other end of a long pole attached to the press, the mule walked around and around in circles, giving the press its power. The juice from the cane trickled into a long, shallow pan resting on a frame atop a wood-fueled fire.

The squeezed cane fell to the ground where it was picked up at the end of the day and loaded onto a sled by my brother and sister and then pulled some distance away from the mill by our mule, Old Kate.

There, we children arranged the squeezed, juiceless cane in neat rows on the ground to dry. In the winter, we fed these dried cane stalks, which Daddy called *pummies,* to the cows.

The person in charge of cooking the juice stirred it with an oversized wooden spoon, making certain it did not scorch or stick to the pan. This process often consumed a full day. The cook always knew exactly when the juice had reached the right consistency and was ready to be cooled. Daddy had bought new, shiny gallon, quart, and pint buckets to hold the syrup. When the liquid was cooled sufficiently and the scum skimmed from the surface, Daddy opened a spigot in the boiling pan and began to fill each container very carefully. Once he had a dozen or so buckets filled with syrup, he would seal each with a lid, wiping away any excess syrup that might have dripped onto the sides of the bucket.

My sister and brother were allowed to go to town with Daddy when he delivered the syrup to the doctors and pharmacists to whom we owed money. These professional people got the best syrup: the kind made from ribbon cane, an extra sweet, extra tall hybrid cane. The mill workers got sorghum syrup as did our family. We loved to pour it into hot, buttered biscuits for breakfast, and sometimes Mama would make syrup cake with it.

When syrup making came to an end, Daddy turned to woodcutting as another means of barter to pay the bills. He had always cut wood for cooking and for heating our home in the winter. Now he started to cut wood for other people. He hired an itinerant man, Fate, to help him. They would go to our backwoods, which we called "the new ground," to fell the trees. Sometimes my brother and I could go with them to the woods: he to pick up and stack some of the lighter branches that scattered and fell as the men worked and I to play and watch from a safe distance.

Daddy would select the tree to be felled. He would take the handle on one end of the saw and Fate would take the other. While they sawed back and forth, a certain rhythm developed as the trunk spewed sawdust. Knowing just when to remove the saw from one cut and move it to another spot on the perimeter of the tree was something they seemed to know by instinct. As the climax of felling came closer, Daddy would often stop, stand back, and predict the exact spot where the tree would fall. Soon the men would yell, "Here she comes!"

Simultaneously, we would hear an unmistakable cracking sound and see the men run away from the falling tree.

Now the tree cutting became a one-man job. At this point, Daddy would go to town to find customers and take orders for the wood that he was not using for barter. Fate would cut the branches from the trunk with an ax, and we kids would drag them away and stack them neatly. Finally, he would split the trunk into logs and the logs into sticks of wood. After Daddy had lined up his customers, he would drive his truck to the woods, and everyone there would help load the wood onto the truck. Then the deliveries began. Daddy was insistent that his customers get a full cord for their money, so he made sure each stack, when unloaded, measured four by four by eight feet.

Selling syrup and wood alone did not bring in enough money to keep us going. Around this time, Daddy was also buying, selling, and trading other goods that contributed to our family's survival.

I cannot leave the topic of bartering without talking about the Watkins Man and other peddlers I knew when I was a child. The Watkins Man, along with the Raleigh Man, the encyclopedia salesman, and the magazine salesman, were experts at bartering, but I think it was the Watkins Man who was the most accomplished of all those who bartered in our neck of East Texas.

I loved it when the Watkins Man came to our house. If we were in the field and I saw him driving down the road toward our house, I would run to alert Mama of his approach. "The Watkins Man! The Watkins Man!" I would yell as I ran home to meet him. As he left, I would go back to the field and watch him depart in his car until the dust it left behind screened him from my view.

Our Watkins Man was about fifty or sixty years old; he was slight and had thinning brown hair. I think he had not always been a salesman, because his skin was brown and lined like that of a farmer. He was a pleasant man, not at all unusual looking except for one peculiarity. He had an enormous growth high on the inside of his right leg, its shape shockingly visible through his khaki clothing.

The Watkins Man would call regularly, perhaps monthly, on the farm families within his territory. He probably had customers in town as well, but since town people lived closer to stores, we in the country were his better customers *and* greater challenges because we often

had no money. This dilemma posed no problem for the Watkins Man, who accepted chickens as payment, placing them in a wire cage attached to the rear of his car. A chicken or two or three were always worth a few of the Watkins Man's manufactured products. He would also accept butter, milk, and eggs—even home-sewn products like a quilt—in lieu of cash. The Watkins Man never left a house without making some sort of exchange.

In his car, he carried with him an endless number of products. He always had a sample case he would bring into the house or onto the front porch if that was where one of my parents decided to do business with him. This sample case held a large variety of spices, flavorings, soaps, shampoos, beauty creams, patent medicines, cough medicines, liniments, hair dyes, insecticides, rat poisons, mousetraps, flyswatters, and assorted other items.

Mama did not like to have to stop her work in order to sit down and listen to the peddler's spiel, but he was insistent, and she usually gave in. She was happy to see him when she was out of her favorite flavoring—pure vanilla extract. His was the very best, she thought. She would not buy anything from him that she considered frivolous, but if Daddy were home, he might buy an exotic flavoring that she would never use, a smelly liniment that Grandma Gammill might rub on her shoulders when her "rheumatiz" flared up, or maybe some fancy aftershave for himself.

The Watkins Man brought news about our neighbors and even news from town where he lived. He loved to gossip, but Mama did not have time for this. I *always* had time to listen to gossip, so the Watkins Man could count on at least one appreciative listener at our house.

One time a peddler who had not been to our house before saw Mama outside in the yard and called to her, "Oh, little girl, where is your Mama?" She would always laugh heartily when she told us that story. At such time, I could discern the tiniest flicker of vanity in her own recognition of her youthful appearance.

Long after the typhoid fever had passed, probably when I was an adolescent, I was looking at photographs of glamorous movie stars, fair skinned and poreless, in an old movie magazine I had found somewhere, and so I asked the Watkins Man, "Do you have anything in your case that would bleach my brown skin white?"

"No," he laughed. "Don't you like having a tan? My daughter and all her friends in town want to be tan. I'll bet they're all out in our backyard this minute sunbathing."

Life went along smoothly—for awhile, anyway—after Mama and my sister had recovered from typhoid, and then, suddenly, a new threat surfaced.

Through the Eyes of a Bootlegger's Daughter

⁓

MY MOST DISORIENTING MEMORY suddenly forced me to look
through adult eyes when I was about nine. I had gone with Mama
and Daddy to visit Grandma and Grandpa in Arbala for an hour or
so. When we came back home and walked in the front door, we saw
at once that someone had been in our house. Our meager possessions
were in disarray. Dresser drawers were open, their contents hanging
out or scattered about on the floor; closets and beds were in obvious
disorder; and even the fireplace had been searched, evident by the soot
left all over the floor. I can remember the confusion I felt—confusion
compounded when I looked at the faces of my parents: Mama's face
reflecting what I first interpreted as bewilderment and then recog-
nized as all too familiar shame and Daddy's face revealing shock, fol-
lowed by furious anger.

What could the intruder have wanted? The house held an old iron
bedstead in the front room where my sister and I slept at night and
where we sat and visited when company came, another bed was on
the porch for my brother, and there was one for Mama and Daddy in
the only real bedroom. There were two old dressers with dull mirrors,
a few hard straight-backed wooden chairs, an "eating table" that also
served as our homework desk, two wooden benches, some coal oil

lamps, a wood cookstove, a kitchen worktable, and a pie safe. Our in-
dividual personal belongings were even more meager.

I close my eyes and am back in the old house looking at the faces
of my parents. I see Mama tighten all over. Beginning with her eyes,
the tightness spreads, visibly stiffening her body. She says nothing.

Daddy is furious; he is cussing and stomping around, and he says,
"That goddamned Bear Tracks. I'll wring his neck! I'll stomp the
son-of-a-bitch to death."

Mama says, "Tice!"

This is not the first time I have heard Daddy refer to the county
sheriff as "Bear Tracks." I see at once the difference in Mama's and
Daddy's reaction to this intrusion from the outside world, although I
do not yet have the words to name it. I can tell that she blames him
somehow, but how can he be responsible for this since he was with us
when it happened?

The years prior to President Franklin Delano Roosevelt's New Deal
were pretty grim years for East Texas dirt farmers like my father, es-
pecially if a man had a family to support, and most of them did. Farm
wives did not work outside of the home and family farm. And con-
sidering the amount of work that waited for them there—carrying
water from a spring or well to wash clothes by hand, ironing with a
heavy flat iron heated over a wood fire to press almost everything be-
cause everything was made of cotton, making all the clothing by hand
because ready-made clothes were not an affordable necessity, and
cooking everything from scratch—it is doubtful that even the most
desperate farm wife could have handled an outside paying job had it
been a possibility.

Only the most stoic and conservative farmer in our sandy land
community was able to do reasonably well. For the most part, the oth-
ers treaded water. My daddy was never one to tread water, and dur-
ing this time he pretty much gave up on farming as a way to make a
living. I once read that sand farms easily but gives back grudgingly. I
think that is what broke Daddy's spirit—having to work so hard for
such a meager return. He began to buy, haul, and sell farm produce
and to trade almost anything. Buying and selling became his business.
Due to his frequent road trips, he spent little time with us at home.
Always in search of a way to make a dollar, Daddy started to bootleg,

using his farm produce business as a cover. He did not actually set up a still and make the whiskey, but he bought liquor in Dallas to bring back to our dry county to sell in surrounding communities and in town.

The repeal of Prohibition in 1933—the amendment that supposedly allowed us all to take wine with our meals—had been enacted. In East Texas, wine was unknown by most, but moonshine was well established, and repeal had no meaning until a legislature had established just what repeal meant in a state, city, or precinct. Entrepreneurs, from Al Capone and the regal Joe Kennedy on down to my bucolic Daddy, explored repeal's highly elastic limits.

Daddy's bootlegging activities caused Mama to live in a constant state of anxiety for his safety and our welfare, but danger and illegality are not quite the same thing as shame. Mama was so ashamed to have him make a living this way, chiefly, I think, because she knew his illicit activities were common knowledge in our dry, supposedly teetotalist, Bible Belt community. Aside from this, I think she had seen enough, or heard enough, of alcohol abuse to know that it is often more prevalent in "dry" places. It could be that she felt a foreshadowing of the alcohol-related tragedy that would befall our family before my brother reached manhood.

When Daddy was home, car lights flashing on our front door would sometimes wake us up at night. Daddy would go outside, talk to the men in the car, and then disappear into the dark, into the trees. Reappearing a few minutes later, he would hand them a paper bag or two, heavy with something. They would hand him something in return. He would then stand by the car and lean into the open window of the driver's side while they all would laugh and talk, speaking words I could not hear. Peering around the window shade near my bed, I could see this transaction going on in the moonlight. A peculiarity of our family is that we do not talk even among ourselves about this open "secret." However, on this day—the day of the Bear Tracks invasion as I would later think of it—my self-delusion was no longer possible.

Daddy leaves us standing there in the middle of the front room of the old house while Mama begs him not to go. He quickly gets into his truck and drives away. When his truck rounds the corner, I say, "Mama, who's Bear Tracks?"

I already know that is what Daddy calls the county sheriff, but I feel compelled to ask anyway. In a rare moment of confidence sharing with me, Mama says, "They were looking for that stuff. I've begged him not to sell that stuff. I've told him over and over this was going to happen someday. And now I don't know what he will do. As mad as he is now, he might try to kill the sheriff, and then what will we do?"

I know she does not expect an answer from me, but at that moment, "and then what will we do?" becomes my worry, too. I can feel Mama's helplessness at facing a situation over which she and I have no control. It is the first time I feel intense shame over something someone else did. Somehow I soak up Mama's shame for Daddy's "transgressions" before I fully understand what they are or what they mean for us as a family.

My sister does not remember the incident. She must have been away at school when it happened, and it is not something we would have talked about after the heat of the moment. However, it is etched in my memory in living color. I know "the color of the silence of women," as a contemporary woman writer recently named it. It is only now that I am beginning to realize how costly silence can sometimes be.

Although I do not remember how that particular situation involving Bear Tracks was resolved (chances are I never heard any more about it), I do know that Daddy did not kill the sheriff or get hauled off to jail. He surely sensed our worry, though, and why he did not try to relieve our anxiety, I do not know. Perhaps he could not get through to Mama and simply gave up trying to make her understand his point of view. Or, perhaps, he did not even try. A "real" man, after all, did not have to explain his actions to his wife in 1939. And since Mama had no way to make a living herself and no parents to go home to, Daddy must have known it was not likely that she would have taken the children and left. Or, perhaps, no matter how much she fussed, he never questioned her absolute loyalty and devotion to him.

His bootlegging activities actually gave us very little material reward. Sometimes we had a few extras—Daddy had his truck—but the risks were high and the rewards meager. More probable a motive than the financial one was that he liked living on the edge, close to danger and always on the move. And besides, the tedium of dirt farm-

ing in worn-out soil, giving so little in return, held zero appeal for a restless, adventurous soul.

I do not think Daddy particularly cared what the community thought about his activities, but he certainly wanted his children to be on their best behavior when they went out into the world. "Be sweet," he would always tell us when we were saying good-bye to him for a few minutes or a few days—advice that has not always served me well over the years, I fear.

Each year as I grew older, Mama's and Daddy's differences became clearer to me, but what that meant for me or why it was so, I did not know. Now I know that those differences, rooted in their temperaments and rearing, began long before I was born. Eventually, I began to see more clearly that I am the sum not only of my own past, as William Faulkner once expressed it, but of the past of my parents and grandparents as well.

Witnesses to the End of the Nineteenth Century

⌒

MY STORY ACTUALLY BEGINS long before my first memories. It begins with my grandparents.

I clearly remember my paternal grandparents, Molly and Tom Gammill. After all, my family lived in the same small house with them until I was almost six years old. However, I do not remember their talking about their life in Tennessee, their home before they came, by wagon, to Texas. I do not remember either of his parents as great storytellers, but my daddy was superb at making the past come to life through his stories. He could even make things he had not actually witnessed sound like firsthand accounts. It was to my father that I had to turn for stories of his parents' lives before I knew them.

A few years before Daddy died in 1984, I had asked him to tape record some of his memories. Among the reasons I wanted to do this was to see if I could come to understand more clearly the origins of the influences my grandparents and parents had had on me. A more compelling reason, however, was that I wanted to feel again, no matter how diluted by the years, the joy and warmth I had always felt when, as a little girl, Daddy took me in his lap and told me stories.

As I prepare to listen to his voice on tape, I can almost hear my child's voice begging, "Daddy, tell me the story about how y'all got to Texas from Tennessee."

And from the tape recorder, I hear *his* voice:

"It was around 1901—I wasn't even born yet, and neither was Clara. Mama and Papa already had Warren, Azz, Douglas, Gardner, and my sister, Lola. It took them three months to travel by wagon from Savannah, in Hardin County, Tennessee, to Arbala, Texas. In Tennessee, they lived on a farm near the Shiloh battlefield, but they didn't own their farm, and that's the main reason they wanted to go to Texas. Some of their folks had already been to Arbala, and they came back and told Mama and Papa it was a good place to make a living. So they packed up and started out, along with Papa's brother and his family. There were two wagons and all the livestock they owned. They had to sleep in their wagons at night and cook everything on campfires. They had to cross rivers and travel on cow paths some of the time. Papa told me when they got to the White River, I think it was in Arkansas, there wasn't any bridge or ferry, like there'd been when they crossed the Mississippi, and so they had to ford the river. Papa got his wagon across all right, and then his brother started across. It was a shallow river, but there were some deep places. All of a sudden, one of the wheels on his brother's wagon dropped into deep water. They had to unload most of the wagon and tie ropes around the wheel to help the horses pull it out of the hole.

"Your Grandma had been through a lot by that time. She'd raised her brothers and sisters after her Mammy died, and then she had her own kids to raise. She told me once she remembered Yankees passing through her Pappy's farm there in Tennessee when she was a little bitty girl. Her Pappy hid in the cellar when they heard the Yankees were coming, but first he shot their best horse so the Yankees couldn't steal it. That was way back in the Civil War.

"Your Grandma was nearly forty years old when the two families started out from Tennessee to Texas. She said that when they came to the Mississippi, there was a gambling boat docked there, and she saw the first drunk woman she'd ever seen in her whole life get off that boat. She thought that was the worst thing she'd ever seen.

"My two oldest brothers remember that trip well. Doug told me that somehow Mama managed to bathe and put on a clean dress every single day of that long, dirty, dusty trip. You know, Mama was always particular about things like that."

"Daddy," my voice prompts on the tape, "tell about the time Grandma called you from the field to see the 'auto'."

"I don't know what year that was for sure, but I was pretty little. I was born in Arbala in 1902, and Clara was born there the next year. Well, one day we heard that old Doctor Long from Sulphur Springs was coming to Arbala in his new car. Two of my older brothers had already seen a car, but I'd never seen one. Nobody wanted to go to the field to work that morning because everybody wanted to see Dr. Long's car. Mama promised she'd watch the road and call us if she saw him coming. As soon as she saw the car, she ran to the yard and started to holler, 'Oh-O-O children! Oh-O-O children! Here comes the *auto*. Here comes the *auto car!*' We threw the hoes down and started to run as fast as we could toward the road. We tore over the corn rows like rabbits in a hurry. I was the youngest so my legs were the shortest, and I got to the top of the hill last. I was just in time to see the tail end of that car go over the next hill."

"Daddy, do you remember that story you told once when we were all walking around in the cemetery at Arbala on graveyard working day, and you noticed a tombstone for that man who once shot Grandpa Gammill? You hadn't known that old man was brought back to Arbala to be buried. Tell that story."

"No, I didn't know they'd brought him there. They must have moved him from wherever he was buried. The last I'd heard of any of that bunch, they'd left this part of the country. That old bastard did shoot Papa once. Shot him right in the back. He got mad at Papa because he claimed my brothers threw chunks of dirt at him as he was going down the road in his buggy. Papa asked the boys about it, and they told him they'd been wrestling after they got done plowing, and then one thing led to another, and they started to throw chunks of dirt at each other in the front yard. The old man was going past the house in his buggy, they said, and some of the chunks hit one of his buggy wheels. Made the old man madder than hell.

"After Papa heard my brothers' side of the story, he stopped by the man's house and told him the boys didn't mean him no harm. But the old son-of-a-bitch puffed up like a toad and wouldn't accept an apology. The next time Papa walked past his house on his way to teach singing school at Arbala, he was sitting out on his front porch with his shotgun in his lap. And the next thing Papa knew, he'd been shot in the back of the head and shoulders. The old man took off for the woods and Papa walked on to Arbala. He wasn't hurt too bad. Old

Doctor Long happened to be at the store that day. He'd been to Arbala delivering a baby and he'd stopped there for a cold drink before he went back to town. He dug some of the buckshot out, and put some sort of salve on Papa's shoulders. The law set out looking for the man who shot him. He'd hid deep in the woods. The dogs chased him, but he wouldn't give up, so the lawmen shot at him. Pretty soon he came running out of the woods, clutching his crotch, and yelling to his wife who was standing on the front porch, 'Oh Lizzie, they've ruint me. I'm ruint.'

"Well, he was 'ruint' all right—he got sent to the insane asylum. He never had treated his family right, and they never had enough to eat. While he was locked up, Mama and Papa wanted to make sure Lizzie and the kids didn't starve to death, so Mama would cook extra and Papa would take it up there to their house. After her husband had been in the insane asylum for about two months, he sent word by one of his boys to tell Lizzie she should look in the sleeve of his old black coat and take what she found there to the lawyer, so the lawyer could get him out of that place.

"Well, the next thing we knew, Lizzie and her boys were driving past our house on the way home from town in a brand-new shiny buggy. They were all wearing new clothes, new hats, and shoes, and they had three sacks of groceries. The next week they left Arbala for good, and I think they left the old man in the asylum while they went back to Tennessee and a better life without him. I don't think anybody felt sorry for him. He'd been so stingy with his wife and kids all those years, and all that time, there lay that money hidden in the sleeve of his old black coat."

Daddy had a deep respect for both his parents. He often talked about how Grandma Gammill could always find something—food, clothing, quilts—to share with a neighbor in trouble. And, although he was not a churchgoing man himself, I think he was proud that his father had an active role in the Arbala Methodist Church. The respect he had for them did not keep him from cussing in front of them, however. One family story tells how he cussed so ferociously one time in Grandma's presence, he made her faint.

Grandma Gammill was a large woman—a little heavy, but not fat. She did not have a soft feminine face like Mama's; it was a stronger, more certain-of-itself sort of face with a determined thrust of the

*Grandma Molly Gammill poses with her glass of snuff,
circa 1941.*

chin. When Grandma laughed, she laughed all over, her whole body
shaking. I do not remember sitting in Grandma's lap to be cuddled—
not because she refused to hold me, but because, like Mama, she had
very little time to sit down. Grandma never sang to me like Grandpa,
nor did she defer to Grandpa like Mama did to Daddy.

After Grandpa died, she took turns visiting her seven children for
a few weeks at a time. I loved when she came to our house. We had a

radio by that time, and she was fond of listening to her favorite soaps, which she called "my stories." If my uncle or one of her other children came to wherever she was at the time to take her to their house for a visit, she would always refuse to leave until her stories were over.

When Grandma was older, and I was a teenager, she always told me, "Stand up straight!" and "Be proud!" I listened, and I did like to please her, but I could never hold such a pose more than momentarily. Grandma received an old-age pension (these were the days before Social Security), and she had a little spare money with which she would buy face cream and hand lotion from the peddler who came through the countryside.

When Grandma visited us in the wintertime, and the two of us needed to go to the outhouse on a cold, blustery night before we went to bed, she would often say to me on the way, "Let's stop here and make a branch," and we would squat there in the darkness to relieve ourselves. It was *our* secret.

I thought about the women in my family when I was trying to discover my own identity as a woman. My father's mother was not related to my mother, of course, but I found myself comparing them because they were so different, not only in appearance, but in the way they interacted with their husbands and other people. I always admired Grandma's sense of pride, her outspoken manner, and her independence. There may have been tensions between my mother and her mother-in-law—after all, she did often come to visit—but if Mama was ever mad at her I never noticed.

My memories of Grandpa Gammill are mostly those from before and shortly after our move from the house we all shared together. He was not well enough to do hard work as he grew older, which was lucky for me because we spent many hours together in the rocking chair on the wide front porch, watching the world go by. He was the one adult in my life who always had time for me. Grandpa liked to sing and read his bible. He never got mad, and he certainly never cussed like my Daddy. It is Grandpa's request for "raw butter" that I most clearly remember. He would say to Grandma:

"Molly, give me some butter for the potatoes."

"Tom, I *already* put butter on the potatoes when I seasoned them."

"But I want *raw* butter," he would respond.

While proximity to our Gammill grandparents gave my sister and

me intimate knowledge of them and Daddy's stories about them af-
ter they died kept those memories alive, we do not have rich memo-
ries of our maternal grandparents. As adults wanting to know more
about our roots, my sister and I have had to work hard to piece to-
gether our mother's story from the fragments we have gathered over
the years. Mama was as taciturn as Daddy was loquacious; however,
her lack of story is not all because of her reticence. Some of it, she
never knew.

Our maternal grandmother, India Pearl, only twenty-four years
old and pregnant with her sixth child (our mother), left her husband,
Lank Lomax, and their five children in Cooper, Texas, in 1904 to re-
turn to the home of her mother, Amanda Cates, in the Bonanza com-
munity of East Texas. They had married when she was just fourteen
years old. While awaiting the birth of our mother, Katie, at her own
mother's home, India Pearl filed for a divorce from her husband. In
the county records of that year, it appears that she wrote the petition
for her own divorce, pledging to raise and educate her daughter with-
out any help from her husband. As far as we can determine, neither
she nor her mother ever took Katie to see her father, brother, and sis-
ters growing up in Cooper. Our mother grew up believing that an-
other woman had come between her mother and father—a woman
on "dope" her grandmother had told her. Whatever it was that had
caused the marriage to break up left so much bitterness between India
Pearl and Lank that Katie would not know her siblings until she was
almost grown and her brother, Everett, drove down to Bonanza to see
her in his new Model T Ford.

When Katie was a toddler, India Pearl married again and went
with her new husband, Ace Freeman, to work as day laborers in the
fields and canneries of Arkansas and Oklahoma. Barely two years
later, Amanda Cates received a telegram from Ace saying that her
daughter, Pearl, had drowned in the Canadian River near Porum,
Oklahoma, where the couple had gone to work in a fish cannery.
Whether her body was ever recovered or where it might be buried is
not known to this day, nor are any of the details of the drowning. How
Katie got back to her grandmother's house is not clear either. Over the
years, I asked my mother about her mother many times. She seemed
to know very little about India Pearl, and I always thought it curious
that her grandmother, who had raised her and whom she called Mama,

Grandparents Lank and India Pearl in happier days,
circa 1900.

had not told her more. If Amanda knew any of the details of her
daughter's divorce or of her death, she did not pass them on to her
granddaughter. Or, if her granddaughter knew any of the details, she
did not pass them on to me.

Mama was always reluctant to talk about anything she did not
know for fact, but once she told me about a vague memory she had
had from the time she was very young:

"I remember a man picking me up, holding me close, and crying
very hard as he ran along a path by a river. He put me in a little cabin
and gave me some peanuts and told me to wait there. I remember
that, and I think that man must have been Ace, and that must have

been when my mother drowned. But Mama (that is, her grand-mother, Amanda) said I was too little to remember. I don't know how old I was, but I do remember that, and that's why I never believed Ace pushed her in the river like some folks in the community said."

I was so shocked to hear her say, even in this roundabout way, that some people in the Bonanza community had thought this was a mur-der that I never asked about it again. No one had ever mentioned this within earshot of me before.

A few months before she died, my mother found in the bottom of an old trunk the telegram Ace sent Amanda on the day of the drown-ing. The date on the telegram revealed that Mama had been four years old when her mother had drowned and proved to her that she had been, as she had always thought, old enough to remember the de-tails of the anecdote about her stepfather.

Until the discovery of this telegram, Mama had not known the ex-act date of her mother's drowning, the circumstances surrounding it, or how the news of her death had reached the Bonanza community. This belated information gave my sister and me the impetus to begin a search for more facts. Perhaps we could come to understand the cir-cumstances of the drowning and discover where our grandmother was buried.

Beginning our search with the exact date of the telegram, June 8, 1908, and the general location of the drowning, the South Canadian River in Oklahoma, we learned from fragments of old newspaper ac-counts (from Henryetta and Okmulgee) that floods during that par-ticular season had been extremely destructive. Railroad trestles had been washed away and telegraph lines had gone down. Several people had been drowned, but we could find no list of the deceased, no death certificate for our grandmother, no evidence that her body was ever recovered from the river, and no gravesite for her. During this futile search for more information about our grandmother, we did come face to face with a truth about ourselves, however. We had each har-bored a secret fear that India Pearl, filled with despair and guilt for having abandoned her other children in Cooper, had jumped into the river of her own accord. That we had never before shared this worry is typical of the way the women in our immediate family had always kept their fears secret. Learning of the flood's devastation helped us both to understand the strong likelihood that her death had indeed been an accident.

Great Grandmother Amanda Cates, circa 1890.

So this was how Katie came to be raised (as an only child) by her grandmother, Amanda Cates, whom she called "Mama," on the farm in Bonanza. Amanda worked her land with the help of a hired man, planted a vegetable garden every spring, and sold butter and eggs to support herself and my mother. Her grown son, Milton, had left home some years earlier to become a retail merchant in Oklahoma. Mama's Uncle "Milty" sent her new shoes and dresses from his store every Christmas for many years, even after she was grown. He was also generous with gifts to his mother, whose husband had died when Milty and India Pearl were still small children.

I always felt badly that Mama did not have her real mother with her when she was growing up until one day, when I was grown, I compared a picture of her with a picture of me at about the same age. In her photo, evidently taken by a professional photographer who drove around the countryside in his buggy taking pictures, she was dressed primly in a little white dress with ruffles, a white bow decorated her carefully braided hair, a little watch pendant was pinned to her dress, and she wore neat-fitting little stockings and shoes. The picture of me (a school photograph) depicts an urchin with a missing tooth, a cowlick, and a limp bow pinned to the top of her head.

It is obvious from a quick glance at the two pictures that Grandma Amanda had dressed Katie, and I had dressed myself. The picture of me was taken when Mama was doing all the farm work by herself. Obviously, she was at the barn milking when I got ready for school that morning. Always ready to adorn myself with anything I thought might enhance my appearance, I was inclined to pin strange articles to my hair and clothing. Desperate for a hair bow, I fashioned one out of the sweatband of Daddy's old hat. There it sat, atop my head, in my fifth-grade school picture.

Our mama sometimes spoke of her grandmother's second husband, Mr. Adams, and of their moving to his house to live, and she also spoke of her affection for, and attachment to, Jesse Adams, his daughter by his first wife. As children, we had always accepted this story without question. As adults, however, we learned through a search of old records that Amanda Cates had married Adams in January of 1920. Now we had to ask why Amanda, who had been a widow for thirty-eight years and was around sixty years old at the time, would give up her home of forty years to move across the fields and marry a man with a half dozen sons to cook for. My sister and I have conjectured that when our mama turned fifteen years old in 1920, her grandmother knew that the young girl needed an education and some status in the community. Mr. Adams had a profitable farm, a good reputation in the community, and a twenty-year-old daughter, Jesse, who was already a schoolteacher. By marrying Mr. Adams, Amanda assured Katie a place in the community, a sister and a guide (Jesse), and a nice house. Mama, in her reticence, had never told us all this, of course, but for my sister and me, the pieces of this puzzle fell into place.

My mama, Katie Lomax, circa 1920.

Our maternal grandfather lived to be an old man. We did occasionally see him, but since Mama had never known him when she was a child, I do not think she felt a particular affection for him. I remember his few visits to our house during my childhood chiefly because he always brought either a paper sack full of bananas or a few pieces of hard candy. I also remember that he carved the names of his parents and the dates of their births and deaths on blocks of wet cement and placed those blocks at the heads of their graves in the cemetery. Even as a child, I noticed that his hand-done inscriptions and the

awkward-looking cement blocks were out of place among the professionally made headstones marking the other graves.

What effect the thoughts and actions of these people who died so long ago have had on me is impossible to know for sure. I do know that my grandparents' lives spanned the bridge between the Stone Age and the beginning of modern Western civilization, and that I am an heir to both an old world and a new.

Witnesses to the Beginning of the Twentieth Century

MAMA TOLD FEW STORIES about growing up as an only child in her grandmother's house, but over the years I learned that she had had close girlfriends within the community and that she had considered her grandmother her real parent, always calling her "Mama." As I was growing up, we occasionally attended homecoming gatherings of the Bonanza community where people who knew her when she was young never failed to talk about what a beautiful girl Mama had been. I could always feel her brighten on those occasions.

After her grandmother remarried and she gained an older step-sister who had been away to college, Mama was sent away to school in Commerce, Texas. As a child, when I wanted to brag on Mama, I said that she had gone away to college, and she always corrected me by saying, "I went to subcollege." Only after I was grown did I realize that the subcollege she spoke of was the training school affiliated with East Texas State Normal College (now Texas A&M University-Commerce). Mama probably went to school there around 1919, when she was about fifteen years old. In Commerce, she shared a small apartment with a cousin. She was in school there for less than two years, I think, before she became lonely for her grandmother and quit school to return home.

As a child, I always thought that living in an apartment with a girl-friend and going to college must be the most romantic thing in the whole world. I was always fascinated by any scrap of information I could learn about this period of Mama's life. I begged her to tell me more, and I spent hours looking through the leaf book she had made when she was a student at the Normal. The leaves had been pressed carefully, and each had been labeled meticulously in her careful hand. The one studio picture of her taken about this time shows a delicate girl with perfect features, soft round eyes and full lips, and a long, soft roll of dark hair falling over her left shoulder and resting on her breast. The dress she is wearing is as delicate and pretty as she is. In spite of my curiosity, I never learned more than this about her education in Commerce. Mama was not a great talker.

Conversely, Daddy had something to say about almost any subject, and he was a superb storyteller. He did not make up stories, but he surely embellished many of them. His favorite stories had to do with his experiences after he quit school at about the age of fourteen and left home to look for work. At some point, I learned to ask for specific stories, and if he left out anything or changed something in the telling, I was as quick to react to such an omission as any modern-day child listening to a favorite storybook tale. For most of my very early child-hood, we did not have a radio, and we had no storybooks at our house. After supper and homework, we lit the coal oil lamp and begged for stories. In the winter, Daddy would sit in a rocker near the fireplace in the front room where my sister and I slept. I was the smallest child, but I usually managed to get the best spot on his lap.

As an adult, I realized that all of Daddy's stories would die with him unless I could capture them on tape. He was more than willing to cooperate.

"Daddy, tell about going to school at Arbala and about what you did after you quit school," I prod.

"We had several grades in one room at Arbala. Our teacher sat up on a platform. The class that was reciting was up on the platform with the teacher. I didn't much like school because I couldn't read very well. Later on, I learned why, but I didn't know then—I just thought I wasn't any good at my books. I didn't want to sit there and look dumb, and all my brothers were working, so I quit school and went to look for work. Mama and Papa didn't want me to quit.

"My first job was picking cotton near Brashear, Texas. Even though Brashear was only about twenty miles from Arbala, I didn't have any way to get back and forth from the cotton patch to home, so the old man who owned the patch put me up in his barn and they fed me. When there was no more work there, I rode up to Cumby with some people who'd heard there was plenty of cotton there. My friend, Bob, was already there. He could pick more cotton than any man I ever knew. I picked for awhile and then I got a job cutting railroad ties in Cumby.

"One of the men cutting ties there told me they always needed young fellows at the Railway Express yards out west in Sweetwater and places like that. Well, I didn't know how I could get there without any money, but pretty soon it came a rainy spell and there was no more work for me in Cumby, so I hopped on the next freight train going west. First, I got work in Wichita Falls, and then finally I got to Sweetwater.

"The man at the Railway Express in Sweetwater told me he would hire me, but first I'd have to go to their doctor for an examination. I'd never had an examination by a doctor. I was healthy as a horse—a big, strong boy.

"The doctor said to me, 'Where are your glasses?'

'I don't wear glasses,' I told him.

'Well, you need to wear glasses. You can't see well enough to read. You'll have to wear glasses if you work here.'

"When the doctor put the eyeglasses on me, it was like everything came sharp and clear. I didn't know I couldn't see well enough to read, and Mama and Papa didn't know it either. If I'd had glasses when I was at school in Arbala, I wouldn't have quit."

As early as I can remember, I loved to curl up in Daddy's lap and listen to his stories about the old days working for the railroad in Sweetwater. This had been his favorite topic when he was feeling relaxed and happy. As he spoke, his expression would soften and his voice would deepen.

"It was around 1917. My job was to help load the boxcars. Sometimes I even slept in the boxcar at night if something needed to be guarded. Once, I had to ride all night in a car with a corpse. None of the other fellows wanted to do that, but since I was the newest man on the job, it fell to me. I didn't sleep much that night.

"Trains passed all night long—never more than an hour, an hour and a half apart. When a train would stop at the Sweetwater station, people would swarm in for thirty minutes or more. And then it would get quiet again inside the station house until the next train came along.

"I was helping the express manager take on or put off express at that time. Every day we would ship several, maybe a hundred, head of cattle out. We always had to leave room for ice when we loaded the boxcar. We might drag out ten or twenty blocks of ice to place in a car depending on what it held. The ice was made in Ft. Worth.

"Everybody would get off work at noon and go to dinner. There were twenty-two or twenty-three cafes in Sweetwater then. We were supposed to wear our caps and badges when we went to eat, so the waitresses would know to give us a discount. One day right after I started, the express manager took me into the Harvey House with him to eat. I wasn't wearing my cap and badge, so the girl charged me one dollar for my meal. The express manager acted like he didn't even know me, so I had to go ahead and pay full price. Later he came up to the waitress and said, 'Give that boy back his money; he works for me.' I didn't forget again."

As a child, I knew most of Daddy's Sweetwater stories by heart, and so I could ask for them by name as I curled up in his lap at night for another story. He had memorized the names of all the railroad stops between Sweetwater and points north, south, east, and west. He still remembered them all when I was a little girl, and he would call them out, on request, just like a conductor. I had never been on a train, and this was about the closest I would ever come to the real thing, I thought.

(One other train memory I cherish did not come from Daddy. One night J. T. and I spent the night at our cousin's house in Sulphur Springs. The family lived near a train track, and several times that night we heard the lonesome train whistles of the steam locomotives calling us. I had never heard such seductive sounds as those the trains made that night. It was all I could do to stay in bed and not run to catch one of them. We lay awake for hours speculating on the destination of the trains and wishing we were on them, headed back to the good old days in Sweetwater with Daddy.)

Daddy's role in World War I (the Great War) was minimal, and we did not know the full story until he told us this the year before he died:

"It was about 1917—just before I turned 16. I was working for the Railway Express out in Sweetwater when an army recruiting officer came in. He looked at me and said, 'Say, boy, how old are you?'

"I was big and strong, and I looked older than I was, and I knew what he wanted. My cousin, Woody, had already left for the army, and I had been working with some boys at the freight yard who were about to leave for the army, and I wanted to go, too. 'I'm seventeen years old,' I lied to him, and he signed me up.

"He signed up eight of us, right there in the Railway Express office in Sweetwater, Texas. He put me in charge of our bunch and put us on a train for Ft. Bliss at El Paso, Texas. When we got there, we were supposed to be examined first thing, but for some reason they couldn't do it right away. They gave us a place to sleep, though. Gave each one of us six-bit meal tickets, too.

"Every day I ordered three eggs, three pieces of toast, bacon, and french fries with my meal ticket. The eight of us were eating better than we'd ever eaten before, but soon my cousin, Woody, turned me in. He told the commanding officer I was only fifteen, and the officer called Mama and Papa and told them where I was. The first thing I knew about the end of my army career was when the officer walked up to me and said, 'Give me your meal tickets, son. You're on your way back home.'

"I gave him the tickets I had left, and then he handed me a train ticket, which I sold for fifteen dollars. I wasn't ready to go home yet, and I stayed on in El Paso for a few more days. Then I hopped a freight and went back to Sweetwater to work for the Railway Express again."

World War I ended in 1918, so Daddy never had a chance to serve his country in uniform. Until I knew the real story, I had always thought that Daddy had deserted the army. This mistaken belief was based on something Mama had once told me when I found her crying:

"What's wrong?" I had asked.

"It's those men who just went into the field. They were looking for your Daddy. I'm afraid they've come to take him away."

"Why?"

"Well, I don't know for sure. Your Daddy left the army without getting a discharge from World War I. Maybe that's why they want him."

I did not stop to see the missing logic in that or recognize that she

My daddy, Tice Gammill, circa 1918.

was probably covering up for one of his far more recent transgressions, which she did not want me to know about. At any rate, I was ready to run out to the field and fling myself between the men and my daddy when they turned and left of their own accord.

"So what did you do when you got back from the army, Daddy?" I prompt.

"I worked in Sweetwater for a few more years, and then Mama and Papa sent word for me to come home. They needed me to help at the home place. I didn't want to go home empty-handed like I'd left, and

Tice Gammill and friend in Sweetwater, Texax, circa 1920.

I'd saved a little money, so I got off the train in Greenville and bought a pole buggy for sixty dollars and a solid black horse for fifty. I bought some new slippers and some kidskin gloves. I looked like I was living high when I rode back into Arbala."

It was on one of these trips back home that Daddy met Mama at a country dance in the Bonanza community when she was about sixteen years old. He asked his friend to introduce him to the pretty girl and was told that he would never be able to "spark" her because her grandmother would not let her go out with anybody.

"Well, we'll see about that," Daddy said.

He managed to meet her that night and to dance with her. He must have turned on all the charm. He was quite worldly compared to most of the other men at the party. After all, he had been working for the railroad in West Texas and had even been in the army for awhile. He was good-looking with dark brown hair, blue eyes, pretty white teeth (Mama always said so), and a ready smile and laugh. Best of all, he exuded confidence, which must have greatly appealed to her because it was surely a characteristic she did not have. True to his friend's prediction, her grandmother would not give her permission to go out with him. He left the next week on the train to go back to West Texas, and she returned to the school she had been attending at Commerce.

Around 1922 Daddy moved back to Arbala from Sweetwater. Mama was then old enough to date without permission. Soon they were going steady. The only detail I was ever able to wheedle out of her about their romance was that Daddy had taken her to dances and pie suppers in his new buggy. Her grandmother sometimes sent Jesse, Mama's grown stepsister, along as a chaperone.

Mama did not tell her grandmother that she was going to marry. Daddy's niece told me a few years ago that he had walked up the hill to his brother Warren's house and had asked his sister-in-law, Clarice, "Would you bake me one of your good caramel cakes? I'm going to get married today."

Mama once told me that she had been visiting back and forth occasionally with her brother and sisters by the time she married. Her brother, Everett, drove down from his home in Cooper, Texas, for the wedding in his new Ford, which he unfortunately ran into a ditch as they were leaving the ceremony.

There were no wedding photographs taken, so as a child, I imagined a wedding picture of Mama and Daddy—a picture that has stayed lodged in my memory. As I saw it, they sat in their buggy while the preacher sat on his horse nearby. I have no rational explanation for conjuring up this particular picture. As a matter of fact, I probably made it up out of whole cloth.

I did ask Mama about shivarees because I had heard her say she and Daddy had had one. I learned that shivarees were noisy mock serenades to newly married couples, and that they were popular in Texas

Tice Gammill and friend sitting on the running board of a friend's car
(year and model unknown) in Sweetwater, Texas, circa 1922.

at that time. After my parents had settled in for the night, young people came from throughout the community. They sang, shouted, and made all sorts of noises. They tried to kidnap Daddy, but he put up such a fight, they let him go. Mama made them some hot chocolate, and finally they went away, still in a party mood.

The newlyweds went to live with Grandma and Grandpa Gammill. They had no money to rent a house, so Katie left her quiet home for her new husband's lively and opinionated household. Most of the six Gammill brothers and sisters had married and left home by that time, but they all visited often. Shy Katie must have been like a little flower, wilting in this blustery household, but she never spoke of any unkindness from the family within my hearing. She always spoke lovingly of her mother-in-law, "Miz Gammill."

After Lola Pearl was born, our parents left the farm so Daddy could work for the Ford Motor Company in Dallas. At some point, he was laid off, and they moved to Greenville to work for the railroad. There, they shared an apartment with another young couple from Arbala. Their second child, Edna Earle, was born in that little apartment. She died there, too, on Christmas day, when she was only a few months old.

Heartbroken, they came back to Arbala to live with Grandma and

Grandpa Gammill again. Mama talked to me about the baby's death just once, and Daddy talked to me about it once after Mama had died. What they told me helped me to understand the basis of some of the tension between them. No one knew what had caused the baby's death. She seemed perfectly healthy when she went to sleep that night. Mama thought it might have been because Daddy was roughhousing with both of the little girls just before she put them to bed that night, and they were "so excited," she told me. Daddy thought Mama might have rolled over on the child during the night, suffocating her accidentally, because, as he told me, "Katie was always such a sound sleeper."

One and a half years after Edna Earle died, J. T. was born, and I, their last child, came along almost three years after my brother. I was born in Mama's and Daddy's bedroom at Arbala on a blustery, cold February afternoon in 1931. The doctor was called from town to deliver me, and my brother and sister were sent to a neighbor's house, far across the meadow. My sister tells me that when they were allowed to come home, Daddy called her into the bedroom and said, "Listen. What's that noise?"

"I don't know," she answered.

"It's a hoot owl!" he told her and then walked over and picked up the bundle in the blanket. She looked down into my face and saw fuzz on my ears and a full head of black hair, but she said she knew I was not a real hoot owl, nor did I look anything like her favorite baby doll. She was six years old. My Aunt Clara always told me I had so much black hair on my ear lobes when I was born, she thought I looked like a monkey.

Until I was twenty years old and needed a birth certificate, I thought my name was Mary Lou. But when I applied for one at the Hopkins County Courthouse, there was no birth record for a Mary Lou Gammill. After a thorough search of the records, the county clerk found the name of Evie Gammill, born on February 11, 1931. We put the pieces of the puzzle together and decided that the old doctor must have been in such a hurry to get back to town after my birth that he did not wait around to see what they were going to name me. Evie was as good a guess as any.

My sister told me the following incident that had happened around the time I was born and seems to capture the spirit of our daddy.

"I was about six," she began, "and I had done something naughty. At least the aunts visiting Grandma that day thought it was naughty, and they also thought I should be punished for it. Since Mama didn't want to punish me for whatever it was that I had done, the aunts laid in wait for Daddy to come to the house from the field. They couldn't wait to tell him that I needed a whipping. He took off his belt, right there in front of them, and led me into the bedroom. He closed the door and whispered to me, 'Now when I hit the mattress with this belt, you yell and cry.'"

Perhaps these tales of my grandparents and parents have shed some light on the times and places in which they lived, on the nature of our families, and on the person I became.

Living in a Wagon Shed

FOR A YEAR OR SO after we had moved from Arbala, we lived on the land at Seymore in the old "dog run house," called this because it had a long, narrow open hallway through its center with two rooms on either side. It had a tin roof and uneven board floors. It was old and freezing cold in the winter, and it looked as if it were about to fall down. It had no screens on the windows, just chicken wire covering them. In the summer, when we needed to raise the windows in order to catch a breeze, houseflies became a problem.

During the summer of 1938, Daddy was able to borrow almost one thousand dollars to build a house using the land as collateral, thanks to a federal agency that had begun to insure loans for home building. He hired his brother, Azz, and his nephew, Allen, as carpenters. They could build the house for that amount of money, they said, only if we tore down the old house and used the heavy oak sills, most of which were still solid, and any other good lumber they could salvage from it. As it turned out, the inside walls were made of long, smooth pine and were also usable to "box" the new house.

We had to have a temporary place to live while the old house was being torn down, so we moved across the road to the wagon shed. It was late summer. We hitched Old Kate, the mule, to a slide piled high

with our household goods, and she pulled them across the road for us. My sister and I liked to walk barefoot in the smooth places that the runners of the slide made on the sandy road.

Daddy hired two local men to help him tear down the old house. Lola Pearl and J. T. had the job of carrying off the old wooden roof shingles. My job was to stay out of the way. My brother and sister carried the shingles the shortest distance they could to dump them, just out of Daddy's line of vision. A drenching rain soon made the dumped shingles wet and smelly, and Daddy made Lola Pearl and J. T. move them again—this time far away from the house site.

The wagon shed, our temporary home, was built like a small barn except that it had no sides, and of course, it had no floors. The middle part was wide enough that the wagon could be driven under it for protection from rain. My brother, sister, and I soon discovered a narrow ladder built into one side of the shed. What fun to go "upstairs" to look at all the old stuff stored there from long ago. We found ox-bows, hand sickles, shoe lasts, and grindstones: all stored up there on loose boards. Fortunately for us, before one of us came crashing through to the ground, Mama saw us, ordered us down, and declared the "upstairs" off-limits.

Mama's "new kitchen" was a narrow shed with a dirt floor on the south side of the wagon shed. It had no sides, but a big cedar tree kept some of the sun and wind from coming in on her when she was preparing meals on her new stove, a borrowed kerosene beauty. We had used a wood-burning cookstove in the old house across the road, but Daddy thought that stove would be too dangerous to use in the wagon shed. The kerosene (coal oil, we called it) cost five cents a gallon.

Mama cooked not only for her family that summer, but for all the workers involved in building the new house. Daddy bought bacon so that she would have more to offer the workers at mealtime.

That summer Mama had planted a nice garden filled with peas, okra, beans, squash, tomatoes, and turnip greens. All morning she gathered vegetables, washed them carefully (particularly the turnip greens, which she washed leaf by leaf several times to make certain there was no residue of sand left clinging to the underside of a leaf), and then cooked until noon. The food she had ready went into a warming oven over the stove. We kids were assigned the job of keep-

ing the flies away from the things she could not cover. She never put
the cornbread in the oven until the men were ready to sit down for
their noon meal. Once they were seated, she put the thin cakes of
cornbread into the hot oven and a few minutes later took them out
with the tail of her apron. The bread smelled extra appetizing in the
open air.

To get ready for nighttime baths, we drew water by hand from the
well across the road right after the noon meal and put it out in the sun
on the south side of the "jack stable," where Daddy kept a breeding
jack. (Farmers in this part of the country during this era used mules
for pulling plows and wagons. Mules are a crossbreed and cannot re-
produce. A mare must be mated with a jack in order to produce a
baby mule. Daddy was able to make a little extra money by charging
farmers who wanted a mule a stud fee for mating one of their mares
to our jack.) The stable was a few steps to the west of our temporary
home, our "camp," and had always been off-limits to children. We all
were afraid of this animal because he had a terrible reputation for
kicking and biting. He was kept locked up in the stable and only oc-
casionally taken out for exercise. When Daddy took him out on Sun-
day morning, he hooked a thick rope from the jack's bit to our horse's
bit and led them around the pasture.

During the time we lived in the wagon shed, my sister was allowed
to help Mama water the jack and sometimes shuck the corn for him.
Every morning he was fed a foot tub of corn still on the cob. He drank
two tubs of water every day. They slid the corn and the water into the
stable through a low half-door. I once asked Mama why his teeth were
so white and shiny. She said it was because he had never eaten grass
or weeds—he had only eaten oats and corn all his life. I was afraid to
go near him.

We heard Daddy telling stories about how the jack had killed a
young horse by grabbing his upper neck, throwing him down on the
ground, and then kicking him in the lower belly. When someone
brought a mare to be bred to the jack, the men would take the two an-
imals to the backwoods, far away from the house where the women—
Mama, my sister, and I—were. This secretiveness about the jack's
mission, coupled with the embarrassment Mama seemed to feel about
Daddy's involvement with this particular money-making scheme, cast
an aura of mystery around these events. My brother, who seemed to

feel no shame about the jack or his mission, was once given permission to go along with the men to watch, and before my sister could stop him, he excitedly told her about it. Being a teenager already, she understood more than we did about sex, and she tells me now that she always felt ashamed when the men took the animals to the backwoods. She says she felt that there were more honorable ways to make money, and she wished Daddy would do something else.

We went around behind the stable for our baths at night, and when we were clean, we called Daddy to carry us to the wagon bed, where we slept on pallets that dry summer. Of course, there were no lights. We could not afford to use more coal oil after having to cook with it, but we had the stars for light. Mama and Daddy slept on an iron bed set up in the kitchen shed. But hot, dry days sometimes brought nighttime thundershowers with a lot of wind and dirt. When that happened, Daddy would carry our pallets and their feather bed to the barn, just about a yard's length down the hill from our wagon shed. There, he smoothed out the piles of corn, and we all crowded into one of the corncribs to sleep while outside it stormed. The barn had a tin roof, and we learned to love the sound of the falling raindrops striking the tin. The smells of early morning, wet sand, and light scent from the trees remind me of that summer.

The new house had its own wondrous smells: new pine, wallpaper paste, and the new clothes we bought for the fall, thanks to cotton stamps. What I remember most about that summer is Daddy's physical presence. I guess he did not want to be away when something as important as house building was going on. Once, he came back from the lumberyard with "wormy cherry" doors the salesman had convinced him were the latest and most modern doors available. Mama took one look at the doors, and back they went on the next truck. She was not about to accept new doors with wormholes in them. Mama shunned anything not plain, and she had never even heard of Quakers. The plain doors that were installed instead of the "wormy cherry" ones are perfect a half century later. This was the only time that summer of the house building that Mama got her way.

This was also the summer I learned that I did not have to be afraid of lightning and thunderstorms *if* Daddy was at home. If he was away from home during a thunderstorm, I hid under a bed or in a closet until it was over. If Daddy was home, as he often was that summer, no

thunder or lightning bolt could reach me. Mama, too, was so content with Daddy home and a new house rising that she actually gained some weight.

It was about this time that Mama used to sing to me: "Oh the moon shines tonight on pretty Red Wing. . . ." I can still hear the tune, but the rest of the words are lost. She also liked to sing: "Put your little foot right here. Put your little foot right here. Take a step to the right and a step to the left. . . ." Mama is the only grown-up I ever knew who could place both her hands flat on the floor and walk without bending her knees.

After the new house was finished, we came home from school one day to find Daddy with his shoes off and work clothes still on, stretched out on the front room bed in the middle of the day. Seeing our Daddy in bed, in the middle of the day, we knew something was very wrong. Mama tried to keep us out of that end of the house, but I found an excuse to walk near the bed, where I saw tears in Daddy's eyes. When he noticed me, he looked away. We knew, even then, that Daddy could not stand to be disabled in any way. Mama would not answer any of our questions about how he got hurt, and she was extra quiet for the rest of the day. Only later did we learn that he had been working with our one mule to move some of the leftover timbers from the old house when one of the beams broke loose and struck him in the groin.

Mama was always protective of Daddy. I remember another incident that happened some years later. I was watching at the kitchen window when a hog knocked him down, and Mama rushed to his aid when she saw him holding himself. Afterward, I smartly remarked to Mama, "He ought to be more careful," to which she replied defensively, "Well, he didn't have any help." I did not have to be told to say no more about it. We were not allowed to be disrespectful of Daddy, not even secondhand disrespectful in Mama's presence.

Guilt by Association

I MUST HAVE BEEN ABOUT TEN when my brother's teasing started to become something I dreaded above all else. He would get my attention, and then he would stroke the top of his left forefinger with his right forefinger and say in a taunting voice, "Shame, shame on Poosie Lou!" He became a spider to me, an insect, spinning his web around me with often no more than a meaningful glance if we happened to be in the presence of our parents or other adults. He perfected his technique to such a degree that he had only to look at me in a certain way and smirk knowingly, and I was trapped again.

He must have just found out about my "secret": the "secret" I only vaguely remembered when he started to outline it in vivid detail for me, but which became more vivid and more real with each reminder. My boy cousin was only two years older than me, which means that we were about six and eight years old when this incident happened. He had come to live with Grandma and Grandpa Gammill after his mother's death and his father's remarriage. He had an older stepbrother who had passed on to him a thing or two he had learned about sex. Of course, this cousin was anxious to practice what he had learned on someone, and since I was the only little girl around, I was chosen.

"Follow me when I crawl under the porch, and I will show you something. Wait until Grandma goes to the front porch to shell her peas, and then you come around to the back and crawl under there," he tells me.

"Is it a surprise?" I ask.

"Yep, you've never seen anything like it before," he answers.

I remember the dirt, sort of a chicken-smelling dirt (not surprising since the chickens roamed freely around the yards and under the porches), and I remember his pulling out his "thing" and making me touch it. Then he tried to make me let him touch my "thing." I pulled away and tried to get out from under the house. Next, I remember seeing Grandma's thick legs, made even thicker with heavy cotton stockings, standing next to the porch under which we had crawled.

"Come out from under there, right now," she ordered.

We crawled out into the light where she waited with a green willow switch. "Whirr, whack, whirr, whack" went the switch as it made contact with the backs of my bare legs. She sent me into the house and told him to drop his overalls so she could get to his bare legs. I do not know how Grandma knew what had happened, but she doled out the punishment in equal shares.

The whipping surely told me I had done something wrong, but I soon forgot about it, remembering only when my brother told me that he knew something shameful about me and that he just might tell when the right time came. He said that our cousin had told him "all about it." He repeated cousin's version of the story, and I took on feelings of guilt that followed me for many years. When my brother had friends over to visit, I always tried to stay close to them, hoping that my presence could keep him from telling my shameful secret. I was miserable sticking close to them, partly because they made it plain they did not want me and partly because of my fear that he would tell on me. How and why I thought my presence in the company of my brother and his friends could deter the spreading of my secret is beyond my understanding now. It was sort of like rubbing hard on a sore toe, making it hurt even more, all the while hoping the pain will disappear. Why I did not tell Mama that my brother was making my life miserable, I do not know except that I simply could not. For one thing, it would have meant that I would have to tell *her* "the secret," and she would have to tell Daddy.

My brother also liked to tease me in other ways—like daring me to do something. If I failed to take him up on the dare, I would open myself up to being taunted for being a "sissy" or a "coward." If I took him up on the dare, I would surely do something I regretted. Once, he dared me to smoke a cigarette. When he saw that I was actually going to do it, he said, "If you dip some snuff and chew some tobacco, too, I will give you fifty cents."

It took him some time to gather it all, but one day he brought it to me and dared me again. I thought the fifty cents looked pretty good, so I started with the chewing tobacco and snuff. I swallowed some, and it made me so ill, I vomited. After that, he was afraid I would tell on him, and he canceled the dare.

A Safe Haven

SCHOOL GAVE ME A PLACE OF MY OWN if not quite a room of my
own. I loved the "little room"; I always felt I belonged there. I soon ac-
quired a best friend with blond Shirley Temple curls, a skinny frame,
a pale round face, and large gray eyes. The opposite of me in appear-
ance, Dorothy brought sandwiches made with bologna, mayonnaise,
and white bread to school for lunch. How I longed for such a lunch
in a crisp brown paper sack. I brought whatever was left over from
breakfast wrapped in a newspaper and tied with a string: usually cold
biscuits split open with some ham or bacon inside. Sometimes as a
special treat in the winter, Mama would take apples or peaches she had
cut and dried on the barn roof the summer before and make little fried
pies stuffed with this fruit for our lunches. My new little friend, Doro-
thy, liked those pies and was always willing to trade a half of a bologna
sandwich on "bought" bread for a pie, but what she loved more than
anything were the tea cakes I brought to school. Mama often baked
these plain sugar cookies at our house, but Dorothy's mother pre-
ferred to buy their sweets in the grocery store at town, so they were a
real treat to her. Swapping lunches took skill and cunning, but I could
always count on trading a couple of tea cakes for a half of a lunch-
meat sandwich. Lunchtime was bargaining time at school, and I made

My school picture, Seymore School, circa 1938.

out pretty well. Only once do I remember being cheated out of something I really wanted for lunch, and the cheater was an older girl from the big room—a neighbor of ours—also named Dorothy. I will call her Big Dorothy to distinguish between her and my special friend.

"My Granddaddy Lomax brought us a sack of bananas when he came to spend the night with us last night, and I have one in my lunch sack," I bragged as I caught up with Big Dorothy on the walk to school that morning.

"Oh, you have a banana, do you? I don't believe it. Let me see," she teased.

"See. Here it is," I replied, feeling important.

At lunchtime, Big Dorothy suggested that the girls from the little room join the girls from the big room for a picnic in the woods. I was excited because I had never been invited to eat with the big girls before. We all went to the woods at lunchtime, and Big Dorothy told us to spread our lunches on the cloth under the tree so we could share them. Before I could reach for my banana, it was gone.

In the little room, I even fell in love. His name was Freddy Burt. He had curly brown hair and brown eyes, and he was always shiny clean. He was very quiet, a little shy, and smart. Once he gave me ten paper valentines, but he never asked me to be his girlfriend.

To make up for our lack of real boyfriends, Dorothy (not Big Dorothy) and I invented boyfriends. We did not only make them up, we carried on a lively, two-way correspondence with our imaginary friends. I had wonderful fun answering my own love notes and then passing them on to Dorothy to read. My "boyfriend" was named Stewart; he looked like the movie star Cornell Wilde and was crazy about me, naturally. Dorothy's "boyfriend" was Jonas, and she decided to make him a famous singer. He was madly in love with her, of course. In one creative note she passed to me, Jonas asked her to marry him when she grew up.

Miss Annie Mae brought us books she thought we would like from the lending library in Sulphur Springs, the nearest town, some ten miles to the north of our school. In about third grade, I was reading them all and begging for more. Finally, she took Dorothy and me with her to the library and let us select our own books. The Sulphur Springs Public Library was then housed in an old church building that had become too small for its congregation. It smelled of must, dust, print, and old books. I realize now that the children's section, housed in the choir loft, was not large, but I thought at the time that this library was the grandest place in the whole world and recognized that I was privileged indeed to be allowed to browse there.

I have the fondest memories of "The Bobbsey Twins" mystery series by Laura Lee Hope. The blond, blue-eyed twins, Flossie and Freddie, and their older twin siblings always got along well with each other, unlike my brother and I. Perhaps that is the way it is with twins, I thought. "The Boxcar Children" books I loved because the children were self-reliant and knew how to "make do" in any situation. Best of all, they had a wealthy grandfather who indulged them.

I loved stories about girls such as *Heidi* by Johanna Spyri, and *A Girl of the Limberlost*. I have carried the lush green images from the Limberlost story in my memory for many years, and Louisa May Alcott's *Little Women* was my favorite of the many Alcott books.

I learned recently that the "Little Black Sambo" book of my era has undergone a name change. The updated version is titled *Sam and the Tigers,* but the tigers still run "faster and faster and faster and faster" until they melt into a "pool of butter as golden as a dream come true." And the comtemporary Sam still eats all the pancakes he wants, just as Sambo of the earlier version did. After more than half a century, I can visualize the page on which I first saw the tigers melt into butter while Sambo sat at the table with a huge stack of pancakes before him.

Dorothy and I would race through the books because Miss Annie Mae gave a prize every month to the pupil who read the most books. I took a much more relaxed approach to reading in the summer.

SCHOOL CLOSINGS

"School's out, school's out, teacher let the monkeys out," children have sung forever on the last day of the school year, but formal "school closings," such as those we knew in East Texas, have been lost somewhere in the distant past. Before World War II and for sometime afterward, school closings continued to be one of the highlights of my life.

If the last day of school was to be around May 30, we would start to prepare our "program" around the first of May. Usually Miss Annie Mae would choose the play for the little room, and the big room kids could choose their own play or other form of entertainment. In such a small school as ours, every single child had something to do to get ready for that all-important school closing when parents, relatives, and neighbors would be invited to see how much we pupils had progressed during the year and to have a rip-roaring good time themselves.

"MisAhMae, MisAhMae," we shouted to our teacher, slurring her name, Annie Mae. "When can we start planning the program?" We asked this question of our teacher at least a dozen times a week every April.

I remember one school closing in particular, although I cannot be positive about the year. Miss Annie Mae had told us that we could

choose from some readings, poems, or songs she had copied for us and maybe even do a little dance.

"Dance? Dance?" the boys shouted between making gagging noises and clutching their throats.

I asked to do "A bird came down the walk" because I thought the poem was funny and saw an opportunity to make people laugh. That Emily Dickinson might also be saying something more serious escaped me, of course.

Someone else wanted to do, "The Owl and the Pussycat Went to Sea." Dorothy wanted to sing "The Good Ship Lol-li-pop." I was instantly jealous that she came up with that. I had not seen the movie in which Shirley Temple sang that song, but wasn't it enough that Dorothy already looked like Shirley Temple?

A shy little refugee from Dallas knew the words and tune to "Pennies from Heaven." I was impressed. Finally everyone had a part. Our finale was to be a dance to the tune of "Put Your Little Foot" because Dorothy's mother had the record *and* a windup phonograph to play it on.

Early in the morning of the long-awaited day, Mr. Jim Sells and some of the other men arrived on the school grounds to build the framework that would cradle a great iron pot over an outdoor fire. They brought plump, dressed hens, corn, tomatoes, potatoes, onions, chili powder, and other good spices to make a "Hopkins County Stew." It was always the job of the men to tend the stew, making sure it did not scorch and that the flavors blended perfectly. A long wooden spoon was used to stir the stew as it bubbled in the iron pot over the fire. As the lunch hour neared and more people arrived, boards were set up over sawhorses and covered with pretty white tablecloths. The makeshift tables sagged under the weight of all the food the women brought: covered vegetable dishes, coconut pies and chocolate pies piled high with meringues, devil's food cake, angel food cake, and a rainbow of salads. The centerpiece dish, though, was always the Hopkins County Stew. We lined up by the stew pot, our spoons and unmatched bowls of various sizes in hand, and knew there would be plenty for all and maybe some left over to take home. Someone would open the fresh, crisp soda crackers and pass them around. We all knew that eating Hopkins County Stew without crackers was like eating cream gravy without biscuits.

After the feast, we pupils lined up chairs outdoors for the audience. The front porch of the school served as our stage; our classroom (the little room) became the backstage and dressing room. Miss Annie Mae announced to the audience that we were ready to begin. Dorothy was a hit in her sailor dress with her little blond curls dancing all over her head as she bobbed and weaved to "Lol-li-pop." Gazing at Dorothy on stage, I became aware of feeling strange emotions I would later come to know as jealousy.

A first grader forgot his lines and burst into tears. The fifth-grade boys made fun of him and everybody else. Freddy Burt stuck his tongue out at me just before he walked on stage. I was crushed. I was up next and took no pleasure in the small chuckles I got from my best two lines of the Dickinson poem: "He bit an angleworm in halves / and ate the fellow, raw."

Even the little room bully took part in "Put Your Little Foot." We pupils were always heartily applauded and thoroughly enjoyed at the school closings, no matter which lines were forgotten or how many broken hearts were left in the wings.

Good local politicians never missed school closings. Knowing that it was the perfect time to pass out campaign literature and shake hands as well as to get a delicious, free meal, every Hopkins County politician from county clerk to county judge was on hand for the festivities at the end of the school year. Even candidates for state offices sometimes showed up for school closings. Dressed in white shirts and straw hats, the politicians always lent a Fourth of July, Yankee Doodle Dandy air to the celebration. They passed out cards that read, "I solicit your support."

Saying good-bye to my teacher and friends until the fall was always a sad time for me. I never looked forward to the long, hot, lonely summers. We scraped the remains of bubble gum from underneath our desks and packed up what remained of unused paper, pencil stubs, and crayons to use at home on a rare rainy day of July or August when we could not work outdoors. As we filed out on the last day of school, the smells of chalk dust, paste, and of oil on the schoolroom floors followed us. Good-byes gave closure to spring and opened wide the door to summer.

A Trilogy of Diversions

⌒

MY CHILDHOOD SUMMERS WERE ENDLESS. One hot day melted into another hotter, breezeless day. School was no longer a refuge. Heaven was finding a place to hide from the chores, reading a book or an old movie magazine I had already read a hundred times, and stretching out under a shade tree to watch and dream upon clouds and make wishes. Books were hard to come by when school was not in session, so I savored each one, never racing through as I had when a prize was waiting at the other end. Often, I had only old radio and movie star fan magazines to look at in the summer. I do not know where these came from, but I looked at them so often the flawless faces of the stars of that era are etched in my memory.

When Daddy was not away from home for an extended time, he issued orders for us to follow every morning when he left to go about his business that day. He always assigned more work than we could finish in one day. My brother's job, more often than not, was to dig up persimmon sprouts in the north field, and my job was to pick up those sprouts and stack them in piles. Together, we were to carry them to the fencerows and stack them there.

There was no end to the work Daddy would assign, no end to the heat beating down from above and rising from below, and no

end to our grumbling about having to do these jobs by ourselves. We resented that Daddy got to go to town and do what he pleased while we had to stay on the farm and carry out his orders. Mama said nothing, but if it were terribly hot, she often called us in when he drove off.

A fun thing to do in the summer was to look for Indian arrowheads on the farm. We had started this periodic search when we first moved to Seymore and someone told us that the Caddo Indians had once lived here. Occasionally my brother would find an arrowhead and add it to his stash. I never found one, and I began to suspect that he might sometimes be planting them so he could once again prove that his vision and detection skills were far superior to mine. Nevertheless, I continued to look for Indian artifacts every summer until I graduated from high school, because the thought that Indians like the ones I saw in the movies might have lived, worked, loved, and ridden on the very ground I walked on was a thrilling, romantic notion to me.

The job I remember most vividly is picking cotton for one of the neighbors, for which we were paid a few cents a pound. Before I got this paying job, my experience with cotton picking was limited to hitching brief rides on the bottoms of my mother's and sister's cotton sacks the first or second year we moved to Seymore, the only year we raised a crop of cotton.

I am back in the field, pulling a cotton sack between the rows of low stalks. A wide strap fits over my left shoulder, front and back, crosses my chest, and supports the trailing white canvas sack that is open at the top to receive the cotton. I extract the fluffy white fiber from the opening in the top of the hard, dry, prickly bolls, certain to have my fingers stabbed, and in one motion, without rising from a stooping position, insert the cotton into the sack with one hand while reaching with the other hand for another boll of cotton.

"Mary Lou, Poosie Loozey, how much cotton have you picked?" my brother was bound to tease. "Look at that! Such a little wad in your sack. Look how much I have. I'll have money to go to the Old Settler's Reunion, and you won't have a plug nickel. Boo-hoo, boo-hoo."

My response to these taunts was to shed the cotton sack right there and attack my brother with my fists. He would grab my wrists and

push me away and down to the ground. Standing over me, he would look down and laugh.

Lola Pearl was always far ahead of us in the rows. She would already have her cotton sack filled and be ready to go to the scales to be praised by Daddy.

In the fall of 1937, the only year Daddy tried to raise cotton, he, Mama, Lola Pearl, and J. T. gathered it all by themselves and stacked it into big piles on the front porch of the old house, where it would remain until Daddy could take it to the gin. It was a dry fall, and the cotton out of the hull was pure white and fluffy and smelled like clean clothes just taken down from the clothesline. It was wonderful to bounce around in. I could bury myself in it right up to my chin before I got scolded for scattering it on the ground. Before he could take the last load of cotton to be ginned at Sulphur Springs where he got the best price for it, Daddy had to go away from home on business. He sent word to Mama that she should send Lola Pearl with the last load of cotton to the gin at Riley Springs (about seven miles away) before it rained. Lola Pearl, dependable and strong, was the logical choice. J. T. would have made the mules go too fast, I was too little, and Mama was far too busy trying to keep things going at the farm. The day before ginning day, Mama, J. T., and Lola Pearl used bushel baskets to load the cotton onto the wagon equipped with wooden sideboards.

Early next morning before full daylight, J. T. went to the horse lot and caught the mules, Jack and Kate. They were old and gentle, and because he always fed them, they let him lead them into the corral. My sister stood outside the corral, on the third rail of the wooden fence, while my brother stood inside and nudged the mules toward her, so she could put the bridles and harnesses on them. She and J. T. then led them to the wagon and hitched them to it. He was ten; she was twelve.

Lola Pearl climbed up on the spring seat across the front of the wagon and took the leather reins in her hands. She held the reins firmly and waited for Mama to bring her a note for the gin operator telling him where to send the check for the bale of cotton. She was wearing striped overalls with a blue denim shirt and a blue bonnet.

Mama made our poke bonnets from whatever cotton fabric she had on hand. Into slots on the projecting rim on the front of the bonnet, she placed cardboard slats to keep the rim stiff. These slats could

be easily removed when the bonnet was in need of laundering. In the sun, Mama always wore her poke bonnet, which tied under the chin and completely shielded her face from the elements. I could be made to wear my bonnet only when the sun was extremely hot.

As she set out on this trip to the cotton gin, Lola Pearl was barefoot because shoes were for school and cold weather. I stood on the front porch and waved good-bye to her. The rest of the story I heard her tell her grandson recently when he was compiling a grandparent's history of the old days for a school project:

"So Mama gave me the note for the gin man, and she handed me a handkerchief with a dime tied into one of its corners. She told me to buy a big spool of number sixty white thread from Mr. Smith at the gin store. She needed it for patching our clothes. We started out at sunrise—the mules pulling the wagon with the one thousand pounds of cotton, plus me and Mama's dime, down the sandy road. I could hear the wagon wheels creaking with every turn. I went zigzagging down three country roads and met only four cars. I got to the cotton gin about ten o'clock. Mine was the first wagon in line at the gin. I got down from my seat in the wagon so the gin man could drive the load under the suction pipe.

"Some men too old to work in the fields were sitting on the front porch of the store. I was too afraid of them to walk past them to get into the store, and so when the wagon was empty, I gave the gin operator the dime and asked him to buy the spool of thread for me. I don't remember much about the ride home except that I felt happy."

I, too, felt happy when I saw the wagon rounding the corner, coming back home. My big sister was back from her grand adventure.

Finally, there came along something I could do well—something that would be appreciated. I was assigned the chore of bringing a hot lunch to my family when they were working "by the day," which meant from sunup to sundown, for a farmer in his fields across Birch Creek Bottom. Daddy was paid one dollar a day when he worked alone; two dollars a day when he brought Lola Pearl, J. T., and the mules to help out.

Mama's job was to stay home and prepare the food that I would take to the rest of the family at lunchtime. Every morning she (and sometimes I) would pick fresh vegetables from the garden, cook for a couple of hours, and then pack a hot lunch of, say, black-eyed peas,

ham, cornbread, fresh tomatoes, and green onions. Into a basket, she placed real plates and eating utensils (not paper plates and plastic forks) and a big glass jug of iced tea, along with the food. It was my job to carry these items to the field a mile away without complaint and without spilling. I often stopped on the way to dream and play, sometimes wading in the cool creek. My daddy, brother, and sister were always happy to see their noontime meal arrive, and they quickly gathered under the shade of the leafiest tree to share the food Mama had sent. I could not resist a little complaining about the difficulty of the journey or the weight of the burden I carried, and they could not resist teasing me for being such a crybaby.

One damp summer, a neighbor's bottom land, which had been planted in strawberries, suddenly began to produce a bumper crop. They were so prolific, he could not keep them picked, and so he hired all of my family to gather the "number one" strawberries for sale. All the others, the culls, which were perfectly good, we could pick and keep for free. That summer we had our fill of genuine, flavorful strawberries—not the plump, picture-perfect, tasteless strawberry of the modern supermarket. How to preserve an abundance of strawberries presented a real problem for Mama. Without refrigeration, we could eat only a finite number of the strawberries before they started to spoil. I walked many times to the store that summer to buy bags of sugar with which Mama would combine fresh strawberries to make jellies and jams. We turned into strawberries that long-ago summer. And, to this day, I still like them.

Summers were never altogether bad, although I hated hard work in the hot sun. I spent more time praying for rain so that I could leave the fields than I spent praying for my soul. Events such as the Old Settlers Reunion were just a few weeks away, and along with Cemetery Day and outdoor religious revivals, they always provided something to look forward to.

OUTDOOR RELIGIOUS REVIVAL MEETINGS

My great escape from summer tedium led me to tent revival meetings, which were announced from every pulpit, by notices tacked on trees, by handbills in the general stores, but most importantly, by word-of-mouth. Excitement infected the community when we learned

that a particularly charismatic preacher would be coming to conduct the revival. Farmers and their families would come in from the fields early on revival days in order to get cleaned up for services that night.

At our house, if there was no cistern water or if the water well was almost dry, we had to carry water from the north pasture spring to the backyard for our baths. There it would stay in the hot sun until it was warmed. Often we bathed outdoors, around back, so no one could spy on us, rather than try to carry the heavy tub of water indoors. Sometimes we children had to share the same tub of water and bar of homemade soap, but we managed to scrub clean, except perhaps for elbows and necks.

If I had a new dress, this was the occasion to wear it, although I was almost certain to be sweaty and dusty by the time I reached the tent. However, near suffocating heat and unpaved roads could not stop a dedicated revivalist. The devil himself could not have stopped me.

Mama and Daddy did not go to church except for family funerals. Certainly they did not go to camp meetings, but I would always find a way. Usually I could find a neighbor willing to take me along with his family. I loved the drama, excitement, socializing, singing, and group atmosphere.

The stars multiplied tenfold in number and brilliance on these nights. Crickets chirped, the full moon rose, and the air sometimes cooled as the darkness closed in. All the ladies fluttered little folding paper fans, trying to stir the stilled air. On the front of each fan, there was a picture of the Last Supper; on the back, were these words, "Hopkins Co. Burial Assn., and Tapp Furniture Co." Babies slept, big kids played tag, and bigger kids found other opportunities. Then it would be time to start the service, and even the crickets would be silenced. "Blessed Be the Tie That Binds," "The Old Rugged Cross," or "Amazing Grace" might be sung by the congregation, or, if we were lucky, by some visiting gospel quartet. The preacher and his family would be introduced and welcomed. Then the preacher would say how happy he and his family were to be there doing the Lord's will and how appreciative they were for the fresh vegetables, milk, butter, and other good food the congregation brought as offerings. (Everyone knew that a preacher's family had limited time in the summer to raise their own food since they were busy going from revival to revival and from community to community. Though few farm families had

spare dollar bills to place in the collection plate, even the most down-on-his-luck farmer usually had a few vegetables he could spare.)

Brother Martin or Brother Royce or Brother someone else would then begin the sermon. Starting perhaps with a scripture reading, he would soon be pacing back and forth in front of the congregation, his voice growing louder and louder, and the perspiration clinging to his forehead, his face, and his arms. With the spittle hovering about his mouth and his shirt soaking wet, he would warn the faithful to stay close to God. Reminiscent of, though not nearly so eloquent as the early Puritan preacher Jonathan Edwards, our preacher, too, would quote from Deuteronomy, "Lest your foot slide in due time."

"Oh, sinners" the tent preacher might begin, and I always knew he was talking directly to me. I knew he could see straight into my heart where all my jealousy and secrets were tucked away, where every instance I had wished someone dead was written in bold script, and where I knew I was somehow responsible for every transgression of my family. This preacher could surely see straight into my heart where all my badness was rolled into a ball.

The preacher always addressed the backsliders in the congregation. I decided I did not fit that category because I knew I had never been baptized, so I did not really have anywhere to backslide to. I was, I decided, just a plain old sinner, but I could not figure out which of the two—backslider or plain sinner—might be worse. I knew, however, with a great deal of certainty that hell was a fearful place from which there would be no return.

"None of us can tell when our next breath might be our last. If you are in a state of sin when you draw that last breath and you are not saved, you will burn forever in hell," the evangelist told us often enough. "Tonight you have a chance to be saved," he never failed to offer.

While the preacher begged the sinful to come forward, the music began softly, "Soft-ly and ten-der-ly Jesus is calling, come home, come home. . . ." One or two persons might rise from the benches and walk forward. Sometimes, depending on how powerful the emotion was running and how charged with electricity the atmosphere was, others might follow. Lined up in front near the pulpit, the penitents kneeled, asked for forgiveness, and were saved.

I remember a time I wanted so badly to be saved, too, but was in such an emotional knot, I could not untie it in time to make the walk

to the front. I folded in upon myself. I was, perhaps, nine. Maybe my sins were too grievous to be forgiven. Besides, I had the uneasy feeling I would be making a public spectacle of myself—something Mama and Daddy would think was silly and an act almost as bad as committing a sin, I think.

Of course, not all revivalists used scare tactics, although they are the ones I remember most vividly. I think I am indebted to those preachers for my penchant in younger days to reach out for and embrace guilt—not only my own earned guilt but also that which should rightfully have been claimed by others. Hey, guilt, hovering out there with no one to claim you, here I am!

Some tent preachers only spoke of how much Jesus loved us and reminded us that we could, simply by accepting Jesus as our savior, be washed in the blood of the lamb. No one doubted the sincerity of the tent preacher for he would be trembling with excitement about the possibility of bringing lost souls to Jesus. He might even break away from his preaching to sing out, "Where he leads me I will fol-low" or "I love to tell the sto-ry."

Some souls were saved at every revival, and before the preacher moved on, there was usually at least one baptism in a pasture pool or stock pond, as some call it.

Witnesses to the baptism gathered on the banks of the pool while the preacher and the person about to be baptized walked, fully clothed, waist deep into the water.

Holding the penitent carefully, the preacher would say the words of baptism and then bend the individual backward into the water until the "sinner" was completely submerged. The people standing on the banks would sometimes shout, "Praise God. Praise Jesus. Hallelujah."

I had been worried about this "washed in the blood of the lamb" business, which I interpreted literally, and so I was relieved to see, at the first baptism I witnessed, that the person being baptized was wet but not bloody. I was never baptized in a pool. Although I often felt my sins should be addressed, my fear of having my head held under water was greater than my fear of unabsolved sin.

Sin was an ever-present revival topic. I heard tales of older teenage boys and young men with bad reputations hovering outside of a certain church house during its revivals to catch packs of cigarettes and

bottles of booze hurled out an open window as a gesture of repentance by the newly saved soul. These stories were hilarious to some in the community and blasphemous to others, depending on the listener's particular religious persuasion. I was pretty gullible, but I recognized such tales as posturing and lies.

Revivals were an important part of my summers, but my church participation was not restricted to revivals. Even though Mama and Daddy did not attend church, as soon as I was old enough to go anywhere by myself, I went to church services in the big room at school on Sundays. I loved dressing up in my Sunday best and interacting with other kids. I also loved the possibility that one of those kids might come home with me after services for dinner, as we called the noontime meal, and play all afternoon or, even better, that I might be invited home with one of them to spend the afternoon.

Sometimes the preacher's sermons made me fold in upon myself and regret that I had come, but my craving for friendship and my desire to escape from the boredom of home and family pulled me there Sunday after Sunday. As for the tent revivals, the promise of drama at the close of endless summer days was a lure I could not resist.

THE OLD SETTLER'S REUNION

As much a part of my summer life as the outdoor religious revivals and far more exciting was the Old Settler's Reunion, an annual event we looked forward to all summer long. We never called it a fair, although, certainly, that is what it was—and more. The Reunion always took place in the Sulphur Springs City Park for one week in July. This gathering had no religious connotations other than what I gave it by fervently praying that Daddy would make it home in time for us to attend. The Old Settler's Reunion was a family affair for us. If Daddy was not home, we did not go. It was that simple. But no number of assigned chores during the day and no amount of sweat could dampen our desire to attend this great event in the evening.

If Daddy had promised he would take us that night to the Old Settler's Reunion, we prepared for our baths just as we would for a tent revival. Mama ironed and laid out our best clothes, we polished Sunday shoes, and my excitement always rose as the hands of the clock ticked off the minutes. Long before dark, I began to scan the

dirt road leading from the highway that led from town for any sign of Daddy's truck. Although his arrival before sundown did not necessarily mean that we would get to go to the Reunion that night, it was a very good sign. Seeing his truck coming up the road sent me into spasms of joy.

Around this time, though, I realized that Daddy could not be counted on to keep his promises—particularly about coming home in time to take us somewhere we wanted to go—and I soon learned to play games with my expectations, hoping that I could soften my own too frequent disappointments. If I repeated to myself the words, "We won't get to go" (all the while hoping we would get to go), I would already be halfway disappointed, and therefore, the fall to complete disappointment would not be so far. If, however, he did make it home and gave the all clear to go to the Old Settler's Reunion, my emotions soared. We dressed, ate an early supper, and drove the thirteen miles to the city park. Sometimes he gave us each a quarter to spend; sometimes we even had more, especially if we had done some work for neighbors and earned a little money. I tied my coins into a tight knot in the corner of my handkerchief. I never had folding money as my brother sometimes did.

As we inch closer to Sulphur Springs, the electric lights at the Old Settler's Reunion trigger anew our excitement, because electricity for our smaller community is still far in the future. And the sounds! The merry-go-round music beckons, the vendors yell, "Hot roasted peanuts—get your peanuts here," adults and older kids shout greetings to friends they have not seen in months, and the sideshow barker steps out of his tent onto a makeshift stage in front and tries to entice us into his tent to see the "freaks": the four-hundred-pound man or the half man/half woman. The attraction could be a two-headed baby or a bearded lady, or it might be man and wife midgets and their full-grown son. This exploitation of "different" human beings elicits no objections from the crowd of spectators and certainly not from me, starved for anything different, particularly if it seems mysterious or dangerous.

Here are the hootchie-kootchie dancers with their made-up faces and high-heeled shoes, whirling and swirling in their costumes of sequins and spangles, colored bright red and yellow and blue. I stand on the ground looking up at the dancers on the stage. The hootchie-

kootchie girls look tired and dirty. Even their eyes look sleepy with tiny gobs of shiny stuff pulling down their eyelashes.

Until I am old enough for bumper car and Ferris wheel rides, I am fascinated with the merry-go-round. Those enchanting horses with flaring nostrils, flying manes and tails, and sleek, brightly colored bodies bouncing rhythmically round and round to the music are even more magical to sit astride than the real-life Shetland ponies waiting at the far side of the park to take kids on a short ride for "only a nickel."

I wait in the cotton candy line with great anticipation, but I am disappointed when my first huge mouthful of spun sugar shrinks to almost nothing after an instant on my tongue.

"Goobers! Goobers! Hot, fresh-roasted goobers! Get your goobers here! Ten cents," yells the vendor. I cannot be fooled. I know they are just peanuts, and we have a barn full of peanuts at home. He will not get my dime.

Daddy treats us all to frozen custards in crispy sugar cones before we start the journey back to the farm and real life. Memories of this special night will have to last until next year and finally will have to be filed away permanently when World War II breaks out and the Old Settler's Reunion is "put on hold for the duration," as are many of the old ways and life as we have known it.

CEMETERY DAY

Cemetery Day was the final component of the summer trilogy of my youth that included outdoor religious revivals and the Old Settler's Reunion. Members and former members of our little community even today still gather at the church and at the Arbala Cemetery on the second Sunday of June to remember our dead with flowers for their graves, to visit with each other, and at noontime, to share the food we have brought from home. Originally, this special day was called Graveyard Working Day. All able-bodied persons were expected to bring rakes, hoes, shovels, and strong backs to clean out the cemetery and make it presentable for another year. Since the advent of "perpetual care" and paid caretakers, Graveyard Working Day has become Cemetery Day or Homecoming Day. Physical work from attendees is no longer expected; contributing to the collection plate is.

I still attend these ceremonies when I can, but it is the earlier version of them that I recall more clearly.

I am about ten and am impatient. Mama is more deliberate than usual while preparing the box of food we are taking to Cemetery Day. The fried chicken must be wrapped to keep warm, the potato salad wrapped to keep cool, the best jar of pickles has to be chosen, every iced tea glass has to be wrapped carefully lest it jiggle another glass in transit, her coconut pies have to be packed lovingly and carefully in their own smaller boxes, and finally, Mama has to get dressed.

The house is hot. We have no electricity—therefore no air conditioning or fans—and the wood cookstove has been radiating heat all morning. Mama is already sweating, although she has just stepped out of the tin washtub holding her bathwater and tried to dry her body with a towel. Damp body or not, she must wear her corset, she thinks. I guess she has to wear it because all the grown women wear corsets when they go somewhere special.

"Mama, please hurry or we'll miss the program. We'll miss everything," I whine.

Daddy has been ready to go for an hour, and so have the kids. Mama has had to do all the work by herself. In the interest of getting off sooner, we are all willing to help her in our various haphazard ways, but she will not settle for a slipshod job, so we must wait.

Finally, we are all ready to go, and we get into the wagon, along with the food, for the bumpy ride to Arbala. Our first stop is at the cemetery to place flowers at our baby sister's grave. Her name is Edna Earle; she was the second child, and she died on Christmas Eve. We say that someday we will buy a headstone for our baby's grave. We always say that even though we know there is no money for a real headstone. We are not going to put up a tacky homemade stone like Grandpa Lomax made and put up for his parents.

Some other people are still walking around among the graves, talking and telling stories. We join them there. I stay close to Mama and Daddy.

"Where is Mandy Cecil buried?" I ask.

"Over by her mother, Cecil," Daddy answers.

I have long been fascinated with this story, and I am hoping Daddy will tell me some more about it. Mandy Cecil had never known her mother, Cecil, who was about seventeen when she died giving birth

to her only daughter. Mandy Cecil had lived some of the time with Grandma and Grandpa Gammill as she was growing up and had been like a little sister to Daddy, who always thought she was so pretty. One day when she was about fifteen, she became very sick with a bad pain in her stomach. When no home remedy seemed to work, the old doctor was sent for. Word came back to the farm that the doctor had gone fishing, but folks were sending someone to find him. Because the word had been slow to reach him, the old doctor was late getting to her bedside, and Mandy Cecil's appendix burst. The impression her death made on my father lasted past him to me. Two beautiful young women, who should not have died when they did, now lying side by side forever in the little cemetery.

Most of the people who had been walking around in the cemetery when we first arrived had already left for the Arbala Methodist Church, only a few yards up the dirt road. There was to be a program of songs, readings, and reminiscences before all adjourned to the grounds for another sumptuous country feast and an opportunity to catch up on all that had taken place since the last time we gathered.

The church is already full when we get there. We place our food on one of the tables outside under a big oak tree and hurry inside to find seats for the program, which has already started. The pretty girl in the purple dress sits by the organ, just as I remember her from the first time I walked to Sunday school with Grandpa Gammill. A young man who had been a community favorite while growing up in Arbala and who had left to become a school administrator in a large Texas city has returned home on this special day to act as master of ceremonies for the program. We have missed the self-introductions of the audience, but as I look around, I recognize almost everyone and can fill in all the little speeches about their successes and hardships since they have been out in the world and how glad they are to be back home again. What I am really interested in, however, are cute boys, and there are a few here today.

A quartet from the community sings, and a fourth-grade girl gives a dramatic reading. Her aunt, sitting in the pew behind us, whispers to the woman seated next to her, "She's been taking elocution lessons from a woman in Sulphur Springs."

"Is that right?" her neighbor responds noncommittally.

Even I, with all my yearning for the dramatic, recognize that the girl may have had one too many elocution lessons.

The preacher's little daughter sings, "Yes, Je-sus loves me." Some of the old-timers give short testimonials about the "good old days" and tell stories about each other.

Daddy gets caught up in the spirit of homecoming and reminiscence and responds out loud from his seat to some of the speakers. Mama has taught us not to speak out of turn in public, and so I am a little ashamed when everyone turns to look at Daddy, although I know full well the rules that apply to the rest of us do not apply to Daddy. I glance at Mama, and she looks like she is holding her breath, certain that he will say something off-color to embarrass us.

In closing, Brother someone says a too long prayer. I try to cast my eyes downward. They will not stay down. I look around. A neighbor boy I used to play with when the big kids were at school winks at me. I cast my eyes downward. They stay down.

The prayer finally ends, and we are dismissed. Now we are grateful to Mama for her careful preparation of our special Cemetery Day lunch. Ours is the most appetizing of all the food spread before us under the big oak trees in the front yard of the church. Mama does not say anything about our impatience.

Cotton Stamps, Socks, and Self-Respect

⁓

"WHEN WILL SCHOOL TAKE UP AGAIN?" everybody begins to ask in August. Whatever date is mentioned is never too early for me. I am *ready* for school when it finally begins in September. Some of the kids will have to drop out for awhile to help with harvest before frost, but since I am "not much of a field hand," as my family can tell you, I know I will not have to drop out—not for that reason at any rate.

I am on top of the world when school takes up again in 1939. I have new cotton underwear, a pretty, new all-cotton dress, new cotton socks, and new shoes that I am allowed to wear the whole first week of school. I will be going barefoot after that until first frost in order to save my shoes for winter. I have a Big Chief tablet, Crayolas, two pencils, no fountain pen yet, and a real store-bought hair bow.

How I came to be so richly prepared for the beginning of school calls for some background, especially for those who cannot know what a crucial role cotton stamps played in the lives of country folks in East Texas before World War II. Franklin D. Roosevelt had been inaugurated president of the United States on March 4, 1933. On March 9 of that year began the "Hundred Days" planning period for the New Deal, which was billed as a "time of relief, reform, and recovery." I was just two years old in 1933 and not concerned about

SCHOOL DAYS 1939-'40

My school picture, Seymore School, circa 1939–40.

government relief programs for the poor. Around 1938, however, I learned that government programs could make a real difference in my life. At about the same time that President Roosevelt became our savior and hero, we had become eligible to apply for cotton stamps. For me, cotton stamps meant I could have ready-made dresses for the first time in my life. Cotton stamps were coupons given to farmers in exchange for their plowing under their cotton or not planting it. So many acres plowed under (or not planted) brought so many dollars in

cotton stamps, which could be used for purchasing only cotton goods. I am sure this program must have been intended to encourage farmers to plant crops other than cotton as well as to reduce the cotton glut, but for me its effect was an opportunity to feel pretty.

Up until the advent of cotton stamps, Mama or an aunt had made all of our dresses, nightgowns, and underwear. Mama had made them from empty flour sacks, which she had softened by washing several times, drying outdoors in the warm sun, and then ironing. Many of the flour sacks had been printed on the outside with polka dots or bright checks, with tiny bright-colored flowers tied in bouquets, or sometimes with little lambs frolicking in green meadows.

Mama could turn those sacks into very pretty dresses, but to have a ready-made dress was such a treat. It was like having a ready-made sandwich—the kind Dorothy brought to school and traded for a handful of my homemade tea cakes. At the beginning of the school year, Daddy would take us all to town in his pickup truck to buy the things we would need for school. In a way, I am grateful now that there were no resale shops in those days in Sulphur Springs—no Goodwill or Salvation Army or secondhand stores. If they had been in existence at that time, I surely would not have had the pleasure of buying something new. We always described anything not secondhand as "brand new." I was in heaven helping to select my dresses from the retail store. For forty-nine cents each in cotton stamps, I once chose two pretty dresses: one in royal blue with a blue and white sailor collar, the other a green and white pin-striped jumper. I was allowed to select one "best" dress for Sundays or occasional school days. I always chose something frilly and pink for my best dress. Once, I had been allowed to select a $1.98 dress. It was the most beautiful garment I had ever seen. Looking at that dress made my whole body react to it. For years afterward, I would have an intense physical reaction when touching a pretty garment I had just purchased. The difference of feel between a new ready-made dress of that era and one made from a flour sack is the same as the difference between a current ready-made garment and a dress from a modern resale shop.

My sister told me recently about her sharpest memory of the cotton stamp days, an incident that brings our plight into sharp focus. "I was just starting to high school and wanted a navy blue corduroy skirt and coral red blouse that were displayed at Levine's in town.

Mrs. Levine saw me staring at them and asked me if I would like to try them on. 'Oh, I can't buy them. I only have cotton stamps,' I answered her. Then she showed me the 100 percent cotton tags on them, and Mama bought them both for me. I was so crazy about the rich pile on the skirt and the rich coral color of the blouse that I took wonderful care of them and wore that outfit all through high school."

Shoes for school also had to be purchased on these shopping trips to town, but, of course, we had to come up with cash for them. Most of the time we had outgrown our old shoes or worn them out by the time school opened after summer vacation, and we would have to go barefoot on this trip. Sturdy oxfords were selected for us, and sometimes we had enough money for Sunday shoes, too. Sunday shoes were usually made of black patent leather. I am sure Mama bought socks for us on these trips to town or ordered them from the Sears Roebuck catalog, but I never had enough socks. My feet grew so fast that my socks were always too small, sliding gradually down into my shoes as I walked. I spent two-thirds of my childhood pulling up my socks.

I remember the beginning of one particular fall when my brand-new clothes lost their newness on the first day of school.

I am so happy walking home from school through the woods this first day after the first cotton stamp shopping trip. Most of the time we walk home after school down the long, dusty road, but on this day one of the bigger kids decides that it would be fun to go through the woods. I especially like the log footbridge across the creek. There the trickle of water is inviting and the foliage is so dense and green, I think I am the Girl of the Limberlost.

Without any provocation, one of the boys starts to pick on me. I try to ignore him at first, but he will not be discouraged. My brother is nearby, but I know from past experience I cannot depend on him to help me, not the way Dorothy could always depend on her brother James to bail her out of any trouble. Suddenly I have had it with this bully who is tormenting me and who had tormented me before, so I jump on his back, knocking us both to the ground. He has not expected me to retaliate, so it is not difficult to get him down, but he is fat, and I know if I wind up on the bottom, he will crush me. I get to my feet first, and while he is still struggling to his feet, I jump on him again, and there he stays, completely humiliated, until he says "Uncle,"

and I let him up. When I get home, I see that I have a jagged tear—not a simple rip—in my brand-new all-cotton dress. My new shoes are a mess, too.

That was my first and only fistfight, other than with my brother. Since I was the winner, I do not know why I never used that ploy again.

I did deliberately try to hurt someone once around this time, and it was a completely uncalled-for aggression. She was two years younger than I and a new girl at school, although her mother had lived in this community before her daughter was born. I had heard some grown-ups whisper innuendos concerning her mother, and then I heard that her "father" was not her real father. Armed with this "information," I approached her and said in a taunting voice, "Shame, shame, I know something about you—something about where you came from."

Whatever possessed me to do that, I do not know. I must have been feeling pretty low in the pecking order of kiddom. But it was her answer that was wonderful, and it taught me a lesson I never forgot. Drawing herself up to her full height and looking me straight in the eyes, she replied, "My mother has already told me everything I'll ever need to know about where I came from."

Those words were more effective than her fist in my mouth would have been. When I think of childhood cruelties, I think of the oft-repeated old chant, "Sticks and stones may break my bones, but words will never hurt me." I said it enough times myself when I was a child, but I always knew it was a *lie*. I knew even then that words were far more powerful than sticks and stones. Some words you never forget hearing like those the preacher's wife said about me when I was ten or twelve.

I have walked about three or four miles to Dorothy's house up on the highway on this particular afternoon. I am barefoot, as I usually am in the summer. When I arrive, Dorothy's mother tells me that they are about to leave for town, and then she invites me to go along with them. They are going to the picture show and will have an ice cream afterward. They will treat me, she says. Oh, joy, I think, a "shoot 'em up" and then an ice cream in Johnson's Air-Conditioned Ice Cream Parlour. I accept immediately. I cannot take a chance on walking back home to get permission because it would take too long, and her family might leave without me. I cannot ask Dorothy's mother to call, because we do not have a telephone, and so I simply say, "Mama won't

care," even though I know full well she would have had me change my dress and put on shoes. The show is great fun and predictable. The ice cream is tutti-frutti. Johnson's Air-Conditioned Ice Cream Parlour is clean and cold. What a perfect day. Then along comes the preacher's wife with two of her children. She stops to talk to Dorothy's mother, but she cannot take her eyes off my bare feet and old dress, and I hear her say, "Humph, I'd never let a kid of mine go to town looking like that."

Her disapproving gaze has already made me shrivel, and knowing that she is talking about me, I am now fully humiliated. I think it is a wholly undeserved reflection on Mama, and I want to shout, "You old biddy, Mama doesn't even know I came to town. It isn't her fault that I went off without my shoes."

But in my world, you do not talk back to grown-ups. Even my recognition that her kids look scrawny and unhealthy and that she is no prize herself does not make me feel any better. I am too embarrassed by this encounter to tell Mama about it when I get home.

Yellow Dogs, Politics, and Racism

TEXAS POLITICS HAD—AND STILL HAS—A BAROQUE FLAVOR, despite its longtime domination by a single party. The expression, "yellow-dog Democrat," which originated in East Texas, correctly suggests that the dedicated voter would favor a yellow dog (or a crushed armadillo by the roadside) over a competent, committed, and blameless Republican candidate. The party machines of the urban northeast were unknown in our part of Texas.

My family's involvement in local government during the thirties and forties was limited to contact with the Hopkins County sheriff and the Hopkins County road commissioner. Earlier, I spoke of Daddy's encounters with the county sheriff, who made recurring appearances during my childhood years.

The election of the Hopkins County road commissioner was always a big deal in our community. A farmer's access to passable roads was of more immediate concern than personal salvation or the preservation of the republic.

Before the advent of farm-to-market paved roads in Hopkins County, some time after World War II, we had only dirt roads leading to the state highways. Although he held an enviable position, the road commissioner was the butt of a standard joke in our commun-

ity that went something like this: One person would say, "They're grading the roads. It must be close to election time again." The other person would reply, "Yep. It's either that or it's going to rain." The inference was that the road commissioner only ordered the roads worked on when his term of office was up and he was running for reelection or that he used such bad judgment, he would order the roads plowed just before a rain which, as everyone knew, would make them so muddy they would become impassable.

Mama said very little about politics, but once I did hear her say that she preferred one candidate for road commissioner over another because he was a mechanic who could fix the machinery when it broke down, which would save the county some money. I do not know if repairing machinery was included in the job description of the road commissioner, but Mama always saw through practical eyes.

The repeal of Prohibition in 1933 was something of a nonevent in East Texas. The widely held assumption was that repeal opened the pent-up supply and demand for alcoholic beverages of whatever potency the prospective consumer might wish.

In fact, with all the possibilities for crime, corruption, and hypocrisy, "local option" became the effective law as each state, or, as in Texas, each county and precinct, gained the privilege of regulating a newly lucrative source of tax income. Every political entity that opted for continuance of prohibition had its own ways of circumventing the law. The establishment of private clubs, where one might consume the alcoholic beverage of choice, and the practice of "brown bagging," where one could take one's own bottle into a restaurant duly licensed for that purpose, were but two of the ways people found to get around this restriction. As far as Daddy was concerned, our county's opting for "dry" status presented an unparalleled business opportunity.

In order to vote in our county, all persons had to show poll tax receipts. The fee for poll tax was one dollar. Twenty-five cents of that fee went to reimburse the county for the cost of holding the election. I later understood that this tax had been initiated to discourage black people from voting.

At election time, Daddy always took Mama with him to the polling place at Arbala although we had all heard him say from time to time, "I don't believe in suffrage. A woman's vote will just cancel out that of her husband." I assume he was confident that Mama would

vote as he told her—thus not canceling his vote—or he would not have encouraged her to go with him to the polls.

Although I did not know the origin of the term "suffrage," I knew Daddy used it in connection with women voting. What the connection was I could not figure out. What did voting have to do with suffering? Then I read in a history book that England had passed the first women's suffrage bill in 1916. Of course, it was not until the ratification of the nineteenth amendment in 1920 that women in this country had the right to vote. For years afterward, many Texans still believed that a woman's place was in the home, *not* in the voting booth. Daddy was typical of such men in his attitude toward women's suffrage. In an old high school Texas history book, I remember reading some disparaging remarks from men in politics who were opposed to women's right to vote.

In spite of this widely held view of women as second-class citizens, only five years after the women of the United States had gained the right to vote, Texas had a woman governor, or, as Jim Ferguson was widely quoted as saying, "Two governors for the price of one." Jim Ferguson had left the Texas governor's office in 1917 in disgrace—he had been impeached—and returned in triumph in 1925 with his wife, Miriam (known as "Ma"), the newly elected governor.

My sister remembers that Grandma Gammill seemed to take more of an interest in politics than our mother did. She remembers seeing Grandma Gammill, wearing her ever-present apron over her dress, sitting on the front porch at Arbala with a visitor around 1932, when the visitor suddenly took a cartoon out of his pocket to show to Grandma. Because Grandma was laughing so hard and even covered her face with her apron, my sister, who had been playing in the yard, ran up to see what it was in the cartoon that had tickled our Grandma so. In the center of the cartoon was a large wooden chair that actually looked like the electric chair my sister had seen in pictures, but this chair was labeled "The Governor's Chair." Ma Ferguson, wearing an apron that looked just like the one our Grandma was wearing, was pulling on one arm of the chair. Pat Neff, her opponent for the governor's race, was pulling on the other arm of the chair. Neff, who was smaller than Ma, had his heels dug in, but he was losing because behind Ma stood Pa, pulling on her apron strings, adding power to

her pull. Ma and Pa Ferguson together were too much for Neff to overcome.

People in East Texas were still talking about Ma and Pa Ferguson in 1938, when I became old enough to pay any attention to that sort of thing, but it was W. Lee "Pappy" O'Daniel and the Light Crust Doughboys singing "Wabash Cannonball" and "San Antonio Rose" who captured my attention. O'Daniel may not have been a sterling governor, but he was a great campaigner. Prior to his election as governor of Texas, O'Daniel had been a flour salesman and the Doughboys were entertainers who had helped him sell his product on a popular radio show. It seemed natural to enlist these popular songsters in his campaign for governor. Their familiar, "Pass the biscuits, Pappy" became the slogan that won the governor's chair for O'Daniel.

I do not remember paying much attention to politicians at the state level other than O'Daniel, although I was always fascinated with the names of Jim Hogg and his daughter, Ima. Jim Hogg was an early twentieth-century governor of Texas and an honorable man, but his name and particularly the name of his daughter were still the butt of crude jokes when I was a schoolchild. Ima Hogg's beautifully restored home in Quitman is now a designated Texas landmark.

Except for President Franklin D. Roosevelt, who had been our national leader during all of the period I was growing up, I did not pay much attention to politicians at the national level, but listening to the grown-ups talk about Texan, John Nance Garner, who had served as vice president of the United States under Roosevelt, was of interest to me. He was called Cactus Jack by newspaper reporters and others who found him to be prickly. While serving as vice president of the United States under President Roosevelt, he was widely reported to have said, "Being vice president isn't worth a bucket of warm piss." When I overheard Daddy telling Mama that story, I thought it was the funniest thing I had ever heard anyone say. It had just the right degree of naughtiness.

The name of Sam Rayburn, longtime member and Speaker of the United States House of Representatives, was familiar, of course, but I never had the opportunity to meet him although my sister did. Mr. Sam and some of his political associates came to East Texas State Teachers College to campaign when my sister was a student there

around 1942. It was a big event, attracting "real" newspaper men from Dallas who invaded the little college newsroom my sister was working in at the time. "They just took over and pushed us aside," she told me, but later she did get to meet Mr. Sam, a memorable experience.

RACISM

A fish does not know it is swimming until it comes out of the water. Although I was raised in the midst of what would now be called the Black Belt, longtime cotton country, I never recognized racism as such except in retrospect.

I thought that the drinking fountain labeled "For Colored Only" in the Hopkins County Courthouse was for Indians. At the movies, I had heard Indians referred to as "redskins." I kept lingering around the water fountain when we went to town hoping that I would get to see a real Indian. The blacks who worked with us in the fields on the farm drank well water from a bucket, just as we did. That they drank from a separate dipper did not seem all that unusual to me, and it never occurred to me that they would be given a separate water fountain in town. Water fountains seemed a real luxury to me, especially if, as rarely happened, the water was ice cold in the summer. And besides, colored was not the word I heard in connection with the black folks I knew.

I never wondered why black children went to one school and I went to another or why they went to one church and white people went to another. As a child, I accepted that this was just the way things were. I knew that rules varied. Daddy followed one set of rules; Mama and the children followed another. Blacks lived in their settlement; we lived in ours.

In 1948, just after my graduation from high school, my take on race began to change slightly. While visiting my sister, who had moved to her husband's hometown of Pittsburgh, Pennsylvania, I met a Pittsburgh native who said to me, "You people in Texas really know how to keep the niggers in their place." It was said as a sort of compliment, but I was stunned by this remark because of its implication that we were oppressors. I would never have been disrespectful to a black neighbor. My parents would never have permitted it. All

the older blacks I knew I called Aunt and Uncle, just like all older people.

When I moved to Chicago after graduating from college in 1951, I was shocked to see on TV the hate-contorted face of a white woman in a suburban neighborhood screaming at some black people, "Go home. We don't want you in our neighborhood. You can't live here— go back to the ghetto." Gazing at that hate-filled face on the screen, I thought, I do not ever want to be like that.

These two incidents, occurring not quite four years apart and happening far away from the Texas of my youth, made me realize that, yes, racism was pervasive in our part of the country when I was growing up. To make matters worse, racism was often so insidious that I grew to adulthood without recognizing that the sense of superiority we whites wore like a second skin was a lie. Some epiphanies are a longtime birthing.

I understand now that the Ku Klux Klan was an omnipresent and threatening organization in Texas when I was growing up, but people I knew in Seymore and Arbala were so busy trying to make ends meet that we were barely aware of its existence. I must have seen the Klan in newsreels at the Saturday picture show when I was fortunate enough to be able to go to town, but I never associated them with anyone I knew.

"Risins" and "Rheumatiz"

WITH THE SAD EXCEPTION OF our family's bout with typhoid fever, we managed to live without doctor or dentist. Home remedies had to suffice unless we were *really* sick—sick enough to be taken to town for treatment or sick enough to have the doctor drive out from Sulphur Springs to our house, as in the case of the typhoid fever.

As a child I did not appreciate the inventiveness of my mother or grandmother when it came to creating remedies for our ailments. Daddy would comfort the afflicted one with a hug, but it was our mama who did the actual doctoring, and her doctoring was not confined to the children.

Mama's remedy for Daddy's deeply cracked and sore thumb and fingertips was to make stalls for the most painful digits, first covering the tips in lard and then wrapping the fingers in clean, white cloth strips cut from worn-out sheets. She would secure the bandages by tying them with string if she had it handy or with very narrow strips of the cloth. Why lard? We often had no salve or ointment. Why strips of an old sheet? We had no ready-made bandages or tape.

And what was one to do with a badly sprained or broken ankle? Walking on homemade stilts was a fun thing to do when I was in fourth or fifth grade. One day, not satisfied with simply walking on

the stilts, I decided that running bases during a pickup softball game would be even more fun. Before long, of course, I had fallen and hurt my ankle. Miss Annie Mae gave me a ride home from school in her car. Mama put me to bed before going in search of clay down by the creek. There was only sand at our place, and she needed a good quality of clay to doctor my ankle. After she returned home, she mixed the clay with vinegar and then patted the mixture around my ankle to make a cast for the injured limb. I could not move until the clay dried. I do not remember how long it took for the ankle to heal, but the pain and the smell of vinegar and wet clay still linger in my memory.

Mama treated bad colds and croup with Vicks salve rubbed into the chest, which was then covered with warm flannel. In some communities, this was called a granny rag, but I believe Mama called it a poultice. A better-tasting cure for bad colds was a drink of hot milk laced with honey and a few drops of whiskey, which Daddy might give one of us on a rare occasion.

Iodine and Mercurochrome, which we almost always kept on hand, were for small cuts or scratches; soot from the chimney could stop the flow of blood when nothing else seemed to work.

For the relief of boils, better known to us as "risins," we made a paste out of sulfur powder and water and placed it on the sores. Until I was twenty years old and my Chicago boss laughed at me for saying "risin" when he pointed to the sore on my hand and asked what it was, I thought that it was a perfectly good word. His laugh told me that I had been set up to be the butt of his joke, so I ran to consult the dictionary for "risin." And lo, it was not there. Sanctioned or not, "risin" still seems like a more descriptive word than boil. It is from a "rising" of the skin.

Most home remedies were widely shared, but I had at least one encounter with a secret home remedy. I always liked to hear Mama tell this story about my secretive cure. When I was just a few weeks old, I stopped nursing and cried night and day. My parents and grandparents tried everything they could think of to find out what was wrong with me. Finally, they gave up trying to doctor me themselves and took me to a medical doctor in Sulphur Springs. He said he did not know what the problem was, but suggested they give me a certain tonic to see if that would help. Mama said they could not get me to swallow the medicine—she could not get even one drop of water

down my throat. Then Grandma Gammill said, "That baby's going to die if we can't get some liquid down her. I want to take her to Jack Lee. He's not a doctor, but he's sure helped a lot of folks around Arbala."

"So it was," my mama told me when I was a big girl, "that we carried you over to Jack Lee's house. He looked down your throat and told us you had the thrush. He told your Daddy to go to the bottom land and get some white oak leaves. He told Miss Emma (his wife) to boil a kettle of water. When your Daddy came back with the leaves, Jack Lee took the tea kettle of water and the leaves into a back room. Then he came back for you and told us to wait in the front room. In a little while, he brought you back, sound asleep. I did not go back there, but someone told me that is where he kept herbs and leaves and roots. I do not know to this day what he did to you, but you started to get well right away. Before long, you couldn't get enough milk to satisfy you."

"Is Jack Lee the only one who knew that cure?" I ask Mama.

"As far as I know," she answers.

"Did the secret remedy die with him?"

"Well, I guess it did if he didn't pass it on to one of his children before he died."

"Didn't anyone ever ask his children if one of them knew his secret cures?"

"Well, none of them ever let it be known to the general public that he'd ever taught them anything about that."

"That's just awful. To think he knew all about curing folks, and now nobody will ever know what he knew. That's just awful."

"Take the trash out to the burning barrel. I want to mop the kitchen floor," Mama said by way of an answer to me.

It was not uncommon for a child at school to have head lice, but our Mama took particular pride in keeping her children's heads free of lice. Imagine what a blow it was to her to have my sister come home from school one day when she was in third grade with a note from her teacher saying she had head lice. Mama said, "My children don't have head lice," and then she learned that the principal had sent my sister around to each child in the whole school so that each one could see what head lice looked like. To this day, my sister remembers how furious Mama was at that principal. While Mama tried to track down the source of the lice, Grandma got busy with a comb and something

that smelled and looked like axle grease. After she had combed out the lice from my sister's hair, she washed her head with lye soap to rid it of nits. Then she washed my sister's pillowcase and sheets with the same strong soap. In the meantime, Mama thought she had found the source of the problem, and perhaps she did because we never had head lice again at our house. An itinerant family passing through Arbala had stopped to work at our farm for a few days on their way somewhere else. My sister had played with their little girl, and Mama suspected that the lice were in their bedding, which was badly in need of laundering.

Bathing regularly was a real struggle for many families without running water, and as a result, itch was a rather common affliction among schoolchildren. Webster describes the itch as "a skin disorder accompanied by . . . a contagious eruption caused by a mite that burrows in the skin and causes intense itching." The home remedy for this was a sulfur paste rubbed into the skin. More than one child at our school had the itch at various times. One surefire way to become an outcast was to show up at school with the itch. Once, I had it on my hands and around my fingers. The girls at school asked what it was. I knew it was the itch, but I did not want to humiliate Mama, and so I said, "Oh, it's just scratches from the berry vines. I was picking blackberries." That night when I told Mama what a clever excuse I had given for the red rash on my hands, she said, "It's winter. There are no berries to be picked in the winter."

Patent medicines were very popular in the East Texas countryside during the thirties and forties. We heard them advertised on the radio, and we saw them advertised in the newspapers and on bulletins posted in various places. Of all the patent medicines widely hawked during my childhood, I remember two most clearly. The first was Black Draught. It was an absolutely awful-tasting medicine—the worst I have ever ingested—and one that Mama relied on a great deal as a spring tonic for her children. The other medicine I remember was named Hadacol. It fell into the broad category of cure-alls. I never tasted this one, but I knew the adults joked about its alcoholic content. As a matter of fact, *most* of the cure-alls contained alcohol. In a dry community, this was not a small consideration.

Medicine shows still occasionally traveled throughout the countryside when my parents were young, but by the thirties and forties,

they had been replaced by peddlers, who sold many other things along with medicines, particularly cold remedies, liniments, and salves.

My grandparents were especially fond of liniments. They believed rubbing this medicine on sore joints was particularly soothing. Rheumatism was an ever-present concern for older persons. It was not unusual to hear one say, "I'm all stove up with rheumatiz."

One teaspoonful of baking soda dissolved in a glass of warm water was Daddy's favored remedy for indigestion. Mama thought that baking soda in water was the medicine to take for nausea. "It will either settle your stomach or make you throw up," she often said, implying that no matter which way it went, you would be better off after having swallowed it.

Mama came to rely on aspirins for some of our recurring ailments when there seemed to be nothing else that worked. My brother often came down with headaches accompanied by nausea when he was young. Mama noticed that these headaches always seemed to come after he had been playing outside in a very strong wind. At that time, she had never heard of allergies, but she knew that his headaches were in some way connected with the wind. Aspirins seemed to be the only remedy that helped to alleviate the pain, but more often than not we had none when we lived at Arbala, and so my sister was often dispatched to walk to a neighbor's house and borrow two aspirin tablets for my brother's sick headaches.

I often had terrible arm and leg pains throughout grade school and during the beginning of high school. They would come on suddenly without any warning. Mama often told me in a teasing way that they were meanness pains or growing pains, but of course, neither of us had any understanding of what caused these frequent aches. Now I suspect that my quickly growing bones were calling for nutrients missing in my diet. Aspirins always gave me relief if I took one or two and then slept for an hour. Thankfully, by this time, we kept aspirin tablets on hand.

Daddy Leaves Home to Pick Cotton Out West

IN 1940, BEFORE WORLD WAR II BEGAN, Daddy was having a hard time making even a dollar a day. He heard that there was work and good money in Arizona, so he headed there to pick cotton while we stayed on the farm. Mama did not know how we would survive until Daddy could send us some money, but she stubbornly refused to sign up for public assistance, which we all called "relief," not "welfare" as it is known today.

Some of our neighbors did not share these same reservations about accepting help from the government. For months, they had been driving (hitchhiking if they had no car) to town once a week to claim their quota of cheese, oleo-margarine, dried beans, flour, sugar, and other commodities. I burned with jealousy; I, too, wanted to hitchhike to town and claim some of that food. It seemed so unfair to me that our mother's pride excluded us from these handouts. I could have gone to the show in town every day for a month and afterward eaten tutti-frutti ice cream cones in Johnson's Air-Conditioned Ice Cream Parlour on what we would have saved by not having to pay for food "they" were handing out free.

To make ends meet, Mama sold eggs, milk, and homemade butter. Making butter was a particularly time-consuming process. For our

home use, she scooped fragments of butter from the churned milk, squeezed out the liquid, and shaped them into a large round ball. The butter to be sold, however, had to be molded into exact sixteen-ounce rectangles. For this purpose, she used a wooden press purchased in town with which she squeezed every drop of liquid and air from the butter. This particular mold left the imprint of a dainty flower on the top of the butter, making each pound she sold a little work of art. She made our clothes from flour sacks and patched our shoe soles using a kit she had bought from the hardware store in town.

Before Daddy left, we had already contracted with the Carnation milk plant in Sulphur Springs to buy our milk and with a local trucker to pick it up and deliver it each day to the Carnation people. Ours was a very small operation, but it brought in just enough money to keep up the house payments. Still, this twice-a-day chore was an all-consuming job for Mama, my brother, and sister. The milk cans had to be scrubbed and scalded; the barn had to be kept very clean and ready for inspection. The pastures had to be kept free of bitterweeds, so the cows would produce only sweet milk, and they also had to be kept free of a certain kind of clover that would produce gas in the cow's stomach and cause it to bloat. We worked hard to keep that clover out of the pasture, because we had already seen what a disaster that could cause. Before Daddy left for work in Arizona, we had had a cow gorge herself on clover and almost die. I remember that she was stretched out on her side in the barn lot as her stomach expanded visibly and she moaned in pain. My parents had tried to keep me away from the scene of this cow in agony, but my growing anxiety had pulled me back, wringing my hands until they ached. It looked as if the cow would explode when Daddy finally took a sharp knife and plunged it into her stomach in just the right spot. The vile smelling gas came rushing out, and her stomach slowly deflated.

The only role I had in the milk production was to go out to the pasture and round up the cows for the evening milking. Sometimes they were not ready to be driven in from the pasture to the barn, and they gave me a hard time, especially if they were finding lots of green grass to eat. One or two cows would always be at the opposite end of the pasture from the other cows. The trick was to get them all started back to the barn at about the same time. If one cow broke away from the others and started to run, I could hear Mama's caution ringing in my

ears, "Don't make the cows run—they'll hold up their milk if you do."
My other problem in bringing the cows in for evening milking was
the distraction of my daydreams. There was something magical
about the woods and spring, just to the west of the pasture, and I often
stopped there to play—just for a minute. These glorious interludes
gave me time away from my brother's teasing and time to indulge my-
self in all sorts of fantasies, but they held up the milking and made
Mama mad at me. I was often startled out of my reverie by the distant
sound of her voice calling from the barn, "Oh, Mary, oh, Mary!"

My main job was to feed the chickens and gather the eggs. We sold
eggs to the one grocery store in the community and sometimes to the
neighbors. Once a rooster had chased me, and after that confronta-
tion, I was afraid of anything with feathers. To this day, I hate ner-
vous, beady-eyed, wing-flapping chickens. I loved baby chicks, though.
Mama kept two or three setting hens, and I was always anxious to
watch as the eggs hatched. To see the little chick pecking its way out
of the shell was always a miracle to me, but to watch it blossom as its
feathers dried out and became soft and fluffy was even better.

In Daddy's absence, we learned that he was not the only one in our
family who knew how to barter. When he was away in Arizona,
Mama bartered for my winter coat. A neighbor girl had outgrown
her coat, a lovely deep green, soft wool, and I was facing a winter
without one. Mama picked a bushel of pears from the tree in our pas-
ture and offered them to this girl's mother in exchange for the coat.
Even though they had no one in their family younger or smaller to
wear the coat, the neighbor woman drove a hard bargain, and Mama
had to give her some milk, butter, and eggs to boot.

This was how Mama managed until finally we began to receive
some money from Daddy in Arizona. We could also buy on credit at
the small grocery store up the highway. "Put it on the bill," we would
say, and the clerk never hesitated because our credit rating at the store
was good. Although the grocery sacks were sometimes heavy and the
walk was long, especially on a hot day, I always volunteered for this
chore. At the least, it meant a reward of penny candy and at the most,
a frosty, ice-cold Coca-Cola in a green glass bottle. As soon as we be-
gan to receive money from Daddy, we would first pay the grocery
store bill, so of course not much was left over.

When a letter arrived from Daddy, we kids were always excited

but not allowed to open it. That was Mama's privilege. The envelope always contained a money order for a small amount and a letter in Daddy's handwriting. Written with dull pencil lead on tablet paper, the short letters always began, "Dear Wife and Babies." Not one of us was a baby now, and my sister was almost grown—already in high school. I do not know how my brother and sister felt about Daddy calling us babies, but when I saw "Dear Wife and Babies" in Daddy's handwriting, I always felt warm inside.

Making ends meet while Daddy was away somehow gave Mama the energy and confidence to do what she had to do to keep us going, and the excitement of his coming home quickened the tempo of our lives. My sister once said of our parents, "Daddy really thinks Mama has to have bossing." Be that as it may, he never seemed to doubt that she would stay the course.

One time-consuming project Mama had going while Daddy was away was making a quilt. She had been saving scraps of fabric for a long time and wanted to surprise Daddy with something she had made. Every night, after working hard all day, she would sit by the lamp and sew the pieces together for the quilt top. Finally, it was finished and in time for Christmas gift giving.

Daddy had left for Arizona in early spring, and it was almost Christmas before he returned. He came home with sleek new boots and some handsome western clothes. Daddy had always looked nice when he dressed up in the khaki shirts and pants Mama had laundered, starched, and pressed with the creases just right, but now he looked like John Wayne. I thought he was clearly the most handsome man alive. I did not think to question how a day laborer came by such a nice wardrobe, nor would I have dared ask even if I had thought of it.

Many years later, after Mama had died, Daddy talked openly and freely about the time he had gone out west to Arizona to pick cotton. It turned out that a man who ran a gambling operation had hired him to set up tents in the fields near the migrant cotton pickers and to drive a truck to and from the tents to transport the workers who wanted to gamble. He did some gambling, too, I suppose. And we all thought he had been picking cotton.

When he came home, he bought us some furniture for the house. I remember in particular a dining room suite with a buffet, table, and matching chairs. We had never had anything so elegant. As a matter

of fact, I do not believe we had ever had anything that matched. Mama seemed to be embarrassed or a little ashamed of our new furniture. Had she guessed what he was up to in Arizona? Or was the new furniture too fancy like the wormy cherry doors he had wanted to install in the new house? I do not know. I do know that I wish she could have let herself enjoy some of the brief times of good fortune we had rather than concentrate on the bare necessities of existence.

I do know now that my parents were as opposite in temperament, philosophy, and style as they possibly could have been. Mama was dependable and steady; Daddy, reckless and searching; Mama, taciturn and careful; Daddy, adventurous and loquacious. What held such disparate people together is not easy to understand, but that year Daddy was away in Arizona, when Mama proved that she could act independently of him and manage to raise us alone, gives us a clue as to why neither of them ever gave up on the other. It has something to do with that enduring, unaccountable miracle of love.

The Smell of Modernization

ALTHOUGH I HAD NO WAY OF KNOWING what dramatic changes the establishment of the Rural Electric Administration (REA) would bring to our lives, I was excited when, during the summer of 1940 while Daddy was still away, workers started to dig holes beside the dirt road that wound around our farm. They then brought in creosoted poles to sink deep into those holes. I knew from the talk of the grown-ups that this meant we would soon have electricity, just like town people. The REA was about to bring us into the twentieth century. All summer I breathed deeply the creosote fumes—the smell of modernization. Soon the wires were strung on the poles, and an electrical meter was installed on our front porch. Following Daddy's instructions, Mama hired a local man to install the wiring in our house, and soon we had electricity. For a long while, we had only bare single-bulb overhead lights with pull chains, no wall switches, and no appliances. (Later, when we got wall switches, Mama and I approached them with a certain amount of caution. We both knew that the electricity would jump right out of the wall switch into any fingers that made contact with it.)

How wonderful to be able to read by electric light. Now we could read at night without straining our eyes. No more kerosene lamps

with dim glow and smoky shades. Mama cleaned the lamps and put them away for emergencies.

However, some chores continued as before. Mama still pressed clothes with the heavy iron heated on the top of the woodstove, and she scrubbed clothes clean outdoors on a washboard (we called a "rub board") in washtubs after removing them from a big black pot, in which they had been simmering over a wood fire. She still cooked on the woodstove, we still bought ice for the icebox in order to keep the food cold, and we still washed dishes in a dishpan. The few electrical appliances that were available at this time were much too expensive for us.

A couple of years after we had acquired electricity, Daddy came home one day with an old Westinghouse refrigerator that a cafe owner in town was replacing with a larger, better one. It had four claw-footed legs and a new round motor that sat on top, outside the box. By today's standards, the refrigerator would be considered tiny and completely inadequate, but how we all loved it. How rich it made us feel. An automatic icebox meant that we did not have to go to the ice house in Sulphur Springs to pick up a heavy block or two of ice, wrap it carefully in burlap sacks to lessen the melt factor, and rush home to the farm and sturdy square box that would hold it—all before the ice had turned back into water. An automatic icebox also meant that we did not have to do without ice when Daddy was not around to haul it home in the truck. An automatic icebox—that was living! On very hot days, I pressed my body up close to our newly acquired, cold, white refrigerator to cool off.

Electricity for the American home had been a given for at least a generation. Why did it take so long to reach the countryside in East Texas? It was strictly a matter of economics. We could not afford to bring it into our community. I never knew how or why the REA came about until quite recently when I read an article in the British magazine, *The Economist,* that shed some light on the genesis of the REA. Some time in 1938, Franklin Roosevelt received a very large electric bill for his house in Warm Springs, Georgia. The power company was charging eighteen cents per kilowatt hour for electricity there. At his home in Hyde Park, New York, he was paying only four cents per kilowatt hour. Already suspicious that the power companies were gouging many rural areas, he now was convinced of it and set out to

convince Congress of the need to establish the REA for the purpose of giving technical advice and low-interest loans to rural communities wanting electricity but unable to afford it. Now, glory be, and thanks to the miracle of electricity, we had electric lights *and* an electric refrigerator. Best of all, though, we had a radio.

What a great escape that radio gave me. I ran home the last mile from school every day to catch "The Lone Ranger" and "Jack Armstrong, All American Boy." When I did not have to go to school, I listened to soap operas like "Portia Faces Life," "Just Plain Bill," "Stella Dallas," and "Mary Noble, Backstage Wife." At night we listened to "Lux Radio Theater" and "Inner Sanctum Mysteries." Daddy loved to listen to boxing matches and "Amos and Andy." Grandma Gammill was a widow at this time, and she liked to visit her children's homes, but she was so dedicated to her favorite soap operas that she would always tell her sons, "Now don't come to get me until my stories are over. If you do, you'll just have to sit and wait, for I won't miss my stories." Grandma often talked back to the characters in her favorite radio shows, saying things such as, "Well, bless, Patt, why are you crying? He left you without so much as a kiss my foot!"

Electricity at school meant some pleasures we had not had before. We could now have social events at night. We could have a radio and a phonograph, and best of all, someone had donated an electrical etcher, a wood-burning contraption with which we drew outlines of animals and flowers on blocks of wood. There were no electric heaters for us, however. We still heated the classrooms in the winter with big, round-bellied wood-burning stoves.

Electricity at the general store meant a much wider selection of perishable foods. Now we could buy lunch meats and cheese, if we had the money. The store owner could buy fresh produce, milk, and eggs from farmers in the community and resell them to others. Best of all, on sweltering hot days, we could have sweet, ice-cold drinks from the bright red box with the familiar white lettering of Coca-Cola inscribed on its side.

Murder or Accident?

WHILE DADDY WAS STILL IN ARIZONA and after the excitement of our acquisition of electricity, events returned to normal. Day melted into day; nothing different and exciting ever happened. Then suddenly, Roy Branson, who ran the general store, shot and killed his new wife, Faye, while she stood at her ironing board pressing clothes. Someone came to school in the middle of the morning to get Miss Faye's two children, a boy and a girl I had hardly had time to get to know since their mother had married Roy Branson and they had moved to our little community from Dallas.

Daddy and Roy Branson had been friends and business associates. One day before Daddy left for Arizona, Roy Branson had brought his wife and her children with him when he came to see Daddy about something. The men went off in Roy's truck and Miss Faye visited with Mama while the children and I played outside. I do not know what the women talked about, but I think Mama must have sensed some fear in Miss Faye and became uneasy herself, especially in Roy Branson's presence or even when his name was mentioned. When Mama became uneasy, so did I.

Early on the day of the shooting, some men from the community drove up in the school yard and began to talk in quiet, serious voices

to our teacher and then drove away with the two children. The day was exciting in its difference but worrisome. I became agitated and started to worry that my Daddy was somehow involved. From Mama I had picked up this habit of connecting Daddy to unsettling happenings in the world beyond our family.

I went home sick in the middle of the day and told Mama what I had just heard at school, "Miss Faye's dead. Roy Branson shot her accidentally."

Mama said she was afraid something like that was going to happen.

"It was an accident. My teacher said it was an accident," I answered.

Mama said she wished Daddy would not have anything to do with Roy Branson because there were plenty of people in the community who thought that that man had killed his first wife, Billie Sue. All his first wife's sisters thought so, Mama told me.

"When did that happen?" I asked.

Mama said that it happened a long time ago before we moved to Seymore. According to her sisters, Billie Sue was about to have a baby, and Roy Branson would not let them come to be with her when she was about to deliver. Finally, Roy let his wife's sister-in-law come to help with the delivery, and after she went home, his wife died.

"Died? Did having the baby kill her?" I asked.

Mama told me no, it was not like that. His sister-in-law said the woman was perfectly all right when she left the house. All the sisters thought he might have poisoned his wife because they knew there had been some rat poison in the house.

I knew Mama never carried tales, and I could hardly believe she was telling me this. If what the sisters told Mama had happened was actually true, I thought, surely someone would have reported it, and he would have been arrested. But Mama would not talk about it anymore. There was no more to be learned from Mama about the mysterious circumstances that clouded the case. And of course, I could not ask Billie Sue's relatives, our neighbors, such a question.

Roy Branson had moved to Dallas after the death of his first wife and stayed there while his son was growing up. He had come back to run the general store at about the same time we moved to Seymore. He had married again, and now this tragedy.

When the case came to trial, Roy claimed that the shooting was accidental—he had been cleaning his gun when it suddenly dis-

charged. "Accidental or not" was the prime topic of discussion for months among the adults in Seymore.

"Well, I don't know if he's guilty of cold-blooded murder or not, but I'd vote to hang him on general principles," said our hired man to Daddy one day in the winter when they were cutting wood.

Rumors, such as the following, began to circulate through the community grapevine. Miss Faye was worth a lot of money, and under the Texas community property law, half of everything she had once owned would now belong to her widower. Roy had taken out a large life insurance policy on Faye when they got married. Roy had somehow been responsible for the death of his first wife, and, considering that, it was just too much of a coincidence to think that the death of his second wife was accidental.

The first trial ended with a hung jury, and then we heard more shocking news. While awaiting a new trial, Roy Branson suddenly died. Gossip had it that he had committed suicide in his jail cell.

The two children never came back to school. We heard that their aunt and uncle from Dallas had come to get them and to take their mother back there for burial. After all these years, I still think about those two children I never had the chance to get to know.

The shooting was a terribly unnerving event for our community. We went from nothing ever happening to the worst of happenings in an instant. I have always been one to pick up on other people's feelings, and I began to feel nervous and worried all the time, always awaiting the next bad happening.

After the deaths, a terrible grass fire broke out in a pasture next to the front yard of the school. Soon the yard itself was on fire, threatening to burn our wooden schoolhouse to the ground. We all went out to fight the fire: big kids, little kids, and our two teachers. We had no telephone to call for help or a fire department to respond. Neighbors who saw the fire came running to fight it, and somehow we managed to squelch it before it reached the school building and the outhouses. To me, the fire seemed symbolic of the community's need to cleanse itself after the tragedy.

Sounds of War

GREAT EVENTS SWEPT OVER HOPKINS COUNTY, TEXAS, before, during, and after World War II with a gradualism that Europe would have envied: no revolutions, no scourge of war, no mass starvation.

How long did it take the sounds of war to reach an isolated East Texas farm community in 1941? Not so long if you owned a radio. We still were not receiving a daily newspaper at our house, but in its absence, our radio was our link to the outside world.

"Faraway places with strange sounding names" is part of a line from a song not yet penned in 1941, yet these words accurately describe the first sounds of war to me. I was just beginning to study geography in school and to realize that there was a larger and more exciting world out there somewhere.

I picked up many of my feelings of tension about world unrest from the grown-ups around me, but they were all vague and shapeless and had no face until the events of Pearl Harbor on December 7, 1941. On that day, war suddenly *had* a face even in the most remote regions of our country. We in the countryside of East Texas learned what had happened at Pearl Harbor from the radio, of course, as did the rest of the world.

"Goddamm Japs," Daddy said.

"Tice!" Mama scolded.

We also learned of the attack from the talk of the neighbors: in the fields, at the store, in town, everywhere. I started to imagine that planes would swoop out of the air over our farmhouse and with guns blazing would set the countryside on fire. I could see it all in my mind's eye—the sky and the earth all ablaze and our running to escape the bullets.

The great radio commentators of this era brought the war close, even to little places that never appeared on maps and that automobiles could not find. H. V. Kaltenborn and Edward R. Murrow and William Shirer, whose voices I came to know better than those of my male relatives, told me things like, "It is estimated that ten thousand have been killed in the invasion of France." At the Saturday afternoon picture show, I could see "The Eyes and Ears of the World" and other newsreels offering frightening visions of war. Ernie Pyle's human interest stories carried in the *Dallas Morning News,* which we now read at school, gave the war still another dimension for me.

Humor may have become overshadowed by many of war's tragedies, but it certainly did not disappear. A few editions of the army's *Stars and Stripes,* which carried cartoonist Bill Mauldin's "G. I. Joe," got passed around at my sister's high school. Sometimes she would bring one of the newspapers home. Mauldin, a great satirist, was in the Forty-fifth Division of the U.S. Army. One memorable cartoon depicts a major and a colonel standing on a cliff overlooking a mountain valley in Italy. The colonel turns to the major and remarks, "What a marvelous view. Is there one for the enlisted men?"

In another famous cartoon, Sad Sack stands looking through stacks of notices on a bulletin board in an army barracks. Finally, he reaches a bulletin at the back that reads, "All men will fall out tomorrow morning at 0500 to cross the Delaware. G. Washington."

Even the realities of war still had to be filtered through my imagination and romantic notions. I was eleven years old in February of 1942. Just as the whole country was revving up for war, I was revving up for adolescence, and I was becoming hooked on movie stars. Somewhere I had picked up movie magazines and a few radio magazines. I looked at them by the hour. I knew the most intimate details

of the lives of Rita Hayworth, Ava Gardner, and Hedy Lamarr. Their perfect faces, coifed hair, and slightly parted lips spoke to me of romance and made it difficult for me to look in the mirror.

I was in love with Cornell Wilde, darkly handsome movie idol of that day. I had sent for his picture and carried it around with me. When I was younger, I had told Daddy that I wanted to marry President Roosevelt or Joe Louis when I grew up, for those were the most famous of the famous names I had heard mentioned in that era. Now I was in love with Cornell Wilde, and I did not tell anyone. My make-believe world was still encroaching on my real-life world, but I was becoming a little more careful about mentioning such things out loud.

Of course, I did not understand the changes going on inside or outside my body or that my childhood was slipping away. I did know that the war was bringing changes to my life. I grew aware of the existence of a larger, far more interesting world somewhere out there and the increasing possibility that I might someday break away from my monotonous, closed existence.

Our schoolhouse faced the highway, and Dorothy and I loved to watch the soldiers driving south in convoys to their training camps in Texas. As the war progressed, increasingly more army camps were built in or near small Texas towns, and more troops drove by our school. Sometimes they would stop by the side of the highway, and if we were having recess, we would rush out to talk to them. Most of them were from places as far away as New York and Pennsylvania. We thought that they were dashing and handsome and would surely want to write to us if they had our addresses. I still remember the disappointment I felt when they would tell us to run and get our teacher. We knew that if they saw our pretty teacher, they would not talk to us. We did not even stop to think that for Miss Annie Mae, walking out to the highway to talk to men would have been far beneath her dignity, nor did we even once consider that we might be in any danger.

Then there were the war bond rallies in Sulphur Springs. People came from all the surrounding small farming communities to the only nearby town to listen to patriotic speeches by politicians and patriotic songs by local talent. Speeches by local boys, our returning heroes, inspired us all to dig deep into our pockets to support the war effort. A war bond cost $18.75, far more than most farm families I knew could afford, but most could come up with fifty cents for "sav-

ings stamps," which we could paste in a book and then, when the book was filled, exchange for a war bond.

The war sometimes gave people who wanted to be hateful a chance to ridicule young men who, for whatever reason, might not be in uniform. "You look like a perfectly healthy young person. Why aren't you serving your country?" someone might say to a perfect stranger.

Another person might complain of the shortage of seats on trains or buses because the military had priority in public conveyances. A person bold enough to voice such a complaint publicly would certainly be rebuked with a scathing comment like, "Don't you know there's a war going on?"

In our little corner of East Texas, the war was not all bad. It had opened defense work to us and opportunities to escape our poverty. Daddy got a job helping to build army camps at places such as Camp Maxie near Paris, Texas, and army air force bases such as Majors Field in Greenville, Texas. We did not ask him many questions about his work, because we knew that defense workers were warned in posters, "Zip your lip. The very walls have ears." I do remember, however, overhearing him tell the following story. In Houston he had been hired as a painter in a shipyard. There, the men had had to pass physical examinations as a condition of employment. Daddy knew he would not pass because of a hernia he had never had repaired. His old friend from Arbala, Bob Wesson, said, "I'll take the examination for you, Tice." He did and passed without a hitch. I knew the story from its happening, but I could never figure out how they had pulled it off.

Although manufactured goods were scarce and gasoline rationed, our family had some of the luxuries of life for the first time: a used electric refrigerator, an electric iron, a butane gas cookstove, and a little spending money. We went to the dentist for the first time and to the picture show on Saturday if we could find a ride into town. Most important of all the changes, we were able to pay off all our debts.

The draft skipped over the men in my immediate family—Daddy was too old, and J. T. was not old enough—but it pulled in cousins and others in our little community. At first, every able-bodied unmarried man between the ages of eighteen and thirty-five went, and then later, if numbers were needed to fill quotas, married men with families went too. Most of the young men in our community did not wait for the draft—they volunteered.

"We'll whup their yellow asses," said one of them.

"It'll be over in two months," boasted another volunteer.

"Well, I just hope it's not over before I can shoot a few of 'em. I'd like to get me a couple of them bastards with *their* pants down," said another.

I did not personally know anyone who died in the war, but I knew of war tragedy, close up. My cousin Ben was MIA and then a prisoner of war, and that caused us many anxious moments, although it *was* Ben who had pulled hair out of my head and stuck it into the head of a clay devil he had molded out of the red mud at Grandma's house a decade earlier. Our neighbor, Ernest Sells—quiet, gentle Ernest— was also a prisoner of war of the Germans. And there was Brodie, a neighbor who escaped war injury only to be maimed by a car accident while home on leave.

"Our boys" came back on furloughs in uniform and with tales of remote places, adventures, and experiences the rest of us could never hope for:

"Bob Hope came to our camp with some of the most gorgeous women I've ever seen in my life. I sat there and I thought, how could that old fart have so many women hanging around him and me with no woman?" said one of the "boys" to a small gaggle of females, me included, gathered around him to hear of his exploits.

The uniforms and the experiences they had had transformed them from farm boys to exciting men in my eyes. What my imagination failed to conjure in the way of romantic wartime relationships between male and female, the Saturday picture shows and my sister's letters from soldier boyfriends filled in.

I could see all the young women of dating age with their hair swept up in curls, their lipstick glistening, and their pearl necklaces sparkling as they hopped into the cars of their fresh-faced soldier boyfriends and drove off. At such times, how I longed to be more than a scraggly adolescent.

Scraggly adolescent or not, I did have one triumph about this time. I had never been singled out for any special praise, recognition, or honor of any sort that I remember until this happened, and so it made an indelible impression on me. I can still feel how delicious it was. I was in the "big room" at school, probably in the seventh grade, when my teacher Miss Nonnie assigned our class to write an essay. I cannot

My school picture, Seymore School, circa 1941. I was about ten years old.

remember having written one before, but I felt challenged and excited by the assignment. From the choices offered in the book, I chose "Our Flag" and started to write. The words spilled out—words I did not even know were there—and I could not stop for recess when all the other kids went out to play. When they came back, I was still writing. If nothing else had happened, this would have been enough—the sheer pleasure and joy I felt losing myself for the first time in writing. However, the next day, Miss Nonnie told me that she had liked the piece so much she had taken it to the editor of the newspaper in Sulphur Springs, and he intended to publish it. I had never dreamed that people like me could write things someone might want to publish. I felt so happy and proud that when it actually appeared in print the

Seymore School, 1942. J. T. is on the far right,
third row, trying to hide his bare feet.
I am on the top row, third from the right.

next week as "Our Flag" by Mary Lou Gammill, seventh grade pupil
in Seymore School, I could not wait to cut it out of the paper and take
it around to all my neighbors and kinfolk, so they could heap praise
on me. I carried that clipping all the way to college—all the way to
adulthood. The last I saw of it, it was yellow and tattered but still in
one piece. The last time I actually read it, I could see that it was overly
patriotic and overly sentimental, but what the heck, I could hear Kate
Smith singing "God Bless America," and it *was* my first taste of tri-
umph. And it all happened in the middle of the war.

One sound of war not heard beyond our school occurred on the
cold day our teacher put some cans of pork 'n' beans to warm for our
lunch in the water pan inside our wood-heating stove. Everyone for-
got about the beans, given to the schoolchildren by a relief agency in
Hopkins County. We were engrossed in our lessons when we heard
an explosion—three very loud pops—a bomb, for sure. Most of us
ran outside as quickly as we could. I had reached the highway before
I turned around to see what had happened. The schoolhouse was not

flattened, there were no bodies lying about, and so we went back inside to learn that the bomb was only the three cans of exploding beans. I was grateful for any excitement, but I felt sorry for our teacher, who had to clean up the mess.

During the war, someone had given our school a radio, and we in the big room claimed it for our own. Listening to the radio was a special privilege a pupil had to earn. This kept most of us on our best behavior much of the time. As a diversion from the books, the radio was the best thing that had ever happened to us. The radio still had a new smell about it when one day we came to school and learned that someone had broken into the building and stolen it. In my daydreams, I made great plans to catch that thief and hang him by his toes. Stealing our radio may have been a simple act of petty thievery for the thief, but for us it was an act of sabotage—a deliberate cutting off of our connection to the world and especially to the war.

Of Sugar, Shoes, and Other Wartime Shortages

GEOGRAPHICALLY AND METAPHORICALLY, Seymore and its inhabitants were far away from World War II, but the shortages caused by our country's involvement in that war were close to home.

Meat rationing did not bother my family as much as it did those financially better off, because we were not accustomed to having fresh meat each day. We did have pork, ham, and sausage, preserved from the last winter's kill, and chicken so fresh that the time between its being snatched from the yard and served on a platter was less than the time one would stand in line waiting to buy fresh beef or lamb. Some of our neighbors liked to hunt game and prepare it for the table. Daddy never hunted, so we never had game like some folks, except for once. My brother had gone hunting with some friends, and he came home with an opossum that he begged Mama to prepare for supper. She did not want to do it because she was not accustomed to cooking wild game, but she finally gave in to his pleading and prepared it. I remember that she served it like a roast with baked sweet potatoes. I could not bear to taste it because I had listened to my brother's story of how he and his friends had "treed the possum," and I could not get the image of the poor creature cowering from the hunters out of my mind.

Lack of access to fast transportation made out-of-season fresh fruits and vegetables a rarity at this time, even on town grocery store shelves. Gardens were a common sight, both in town and country. Even though Mama always had to struggle to raise a garden in our worn out sandy soil, she somehow managed to gather enough vegetables from our garden (and at the invitation from neighbors, to gather their excess of corn, beans, or peas) to can or dry enough of this food to last us through winter. Occasionally we had beef in the winter if a neighbor butchered a cow, but I do not remember my family ever using their meat coupons. Store meat was too expensive.

Sugar rationing, though, did give us pause for thought, so we valued our sugar coupons. We never gave those away. We always had to save sugar for berry-picking time. Mama would can, preserve, and make jelly from the wild blackberries in season to last us all winter. Pears and figs from our own trees and culled peaches from our neighbors' trees also had to be "put up" in the same manner. These methods of preservation called for a great deal of sugar. Dried peaches did not. In peach season, when our neighbors gave us peaches not perfect enough for sale, we would wash and peel them, and then slice them into a large, white dishpan. Next, we would take them to the tin barn roof and spread them out in the hot sun to dry. If a rain shower threatened before they were dry, we rushed to bring them in. If birds came near, we shooed them away. When the peaches were thoroughly dry, Mama packed them into little white cotton sacks, much like the little sacks she made for packaging Daddy's homemade sausage. In the winter, those dried peaches were wonderful in cobblers or in little fried pies Mama made in the mornings for our school lunches.

Mama made the best cakes, cookies, pies, and cobblers in the whole world, we thought. Sometimes our hired man, who was single and regularly ate at our house, brought Mama his allotment of sugar and asked her to make his favorite cake or pie for all of us to eat. Mama always received the best compliments on her desserts, and we always had desserts of one kind or another—sugar rationing or not.

Butter and oleo-margarine were also rationed. We had a Jersey cow whose milk turned into wonderful sweet butter under the spell of Mama's magic, but we could not afford to eat that. She sold that butter, and we bought margarine for home use with our coupons. I remember a margarine that came in a solid, colorless block. It looked

Katie Lomax Gammill, circa 1942.

as unappetizing as lard until Mama mixed it with the capsule of red coloring that came with it. After the white margarine was properly tinted, it had a more appetizing appearance—approximately the color of butter.

Even shoes were rationed. Although this proved less of a hardship on us than on city folks, who were unaccustomed to going barefoot in spring and summer, we still had to have good strong shoes for the fall and winter. We learned to patch our shoe soles using a patching kit from the hardware store. Mama was already an expert at patching our clothes and darning our socks, skills she had learned from her grand-mother.

As the nation mobilized for war production, all manufacture of

cars and household appliances was stopped. It so happened that Daddy had a fairly new car at this time, and he saw in this an opportunity to make some money. Intermittently during the war and for sometime afterward when there still were public transportation shortages, Daddy drove for a travel bureau in Sulphur Springs. He would take in his car passengers unable to get public transportation back and forth from Sulphur Springs and other towns, such as Los Angeles and other cities in California or Arizona. He loved the challenge, excitement, and adventure of this work. When he came back home, he always had stories about the people he had met and the new places he had seen. I loved these stories as well as the exotic food he brought back from his travels. Any food other than what we had every day, I considered exotic. As far as I could tell, his adventures with the Sulphur Springs Travel Bureau never brought much extra money to us, but for me, they were the stuff dreams were made of. I think I got my own lust for travel from Daddy.

At this time, gas was rationed and so were tires. It was not at all unusual to see someone stranded on the highway in a dilapidated car, out of gas. An even more common sight were cars by the side of the road, crippled by flat tires. In the forties, tires still required inner tubes, and the quality of the rubber used in their manufacture was far inferior to that used today. Rare were the drivers who would pass up a stranded motorist in such a predicament. Surely there was as much risk then as there is now in stopping to help a stranger on the highway, but the shortages and the rationing seemed to make most people more willing to help each other.

When Daddy was away from home, we were left on the farm without transportation. This had been the case since I could remember, but it was particularly bothersome to me now that I was an adolescent and knew that town, some twelve or thirteen miles away, held many treasures one could not buy at our small country store, just up the highway.

One day I was desperate for some pretty buttons to put on a blouse Mama had just made for me—a blouse I *had* to wear that night.

"It's finished," Mama said, "but I don't have any suitable buttons for it." Then she went on to other chores, and I could tell that my new blouse, which she had made to button down the front, would remain unfinished unless I could come up with some buttons for it.

In this era of transportation shortages, hitchhikers were a fairly

common sight on highways, but little girls did not hitchhike. I knew that, but I also knew that it was my best shot at getting a ride to the fabric store in Sulphur Springs, where they had hundreds of pretty buttons. I knew that Mama would never give me permission to hitchhike to town, so I told her I had heard that our neighbors were going to town in the afternoon, and I would catch a ride with them. Of course, I was lying. I had heard no such thing. I started out, not quite knowing how I would get to Sulphur Springs, but determined I *would* get there.

As soon as I got to the highway, I came across a neighbor boy, Melvin, who was grazing some cattle by the side of the road. I told him I was going to town. He gave me some money and asked me to bring him candy, which I agreed to do. I walked on down the highway and put out my thumb. Soon a car stopped. Luckily for me, the driver was nonthreatening and not a neighbor who would tell on me. He gave me a lift to town, and I found the buttons I needed. I bought the boy's candy and then started to worry about how I would get back to the farm. I walked down to the Trailways bus station and learned that there would not be another bus going in my direction until the next day. I knew I could walk twelve miles if I had to, but I was not eager to do that. Fortunately, while walking around the town square, I came across a neighbor who lived just up the dirt road from us, and he offered to give me a lift home. I knew he would take me all the way to our front door. Now, I had only one problem. How would I get Melvin's candy and his change back to him if I were in a car with this neighbor? I could not ask him to stop by the side of the highway while I talked to a boy. He would think we were sweethearts, and I would be teased forever about having a boyfriend. I devised a plan. I would place Melvin's change in the paper bag with his candy and would throw it to him out of the window of the car as we drove by the place where he was grazing the cows. I did just that, and I was pleased with this ingenious solution, even though I knew Melvin would probably have shared some of the candy with me had I presented it to him in a civilized manner. When I walked into my house with the buttons, I saw that my Granddaddy Lomax had visited Mama and had left me a bag of candy. I was happily munching on that candy when Melvin appeared at our front door and asked me for his change.

"I put it in the sack with the candy," I told Melvin.

"Well, it wasn't there when you throwed it to me," he replied.

"Yes, it was!"

"No, it wasn't. You bought candy for yourself with it."

"No, I didn't buy candy for myself," I answered with the candy stuffed in my mouth.

Melvin then left my house to go back to his cows, and even though I knew the change was in the sack when I flung it out the car window, I still felt guilty. I knew it was my fault that he had no change, but I had no money to give him. Recently, I saw Melvin at a school reunion and told him the story about the candy. After all those years of worrying that he thought I was guilty of stealing his candy money, he did not even remember it. So much for my introduction to ingenuity, partial success, and circumstantial evidence.

No new housing was going up during this time because builders and building supplies were needed to support the war effort. Many people had to double up in apartments and houses, particularly in towns with nearby military bases or defense plants. Again, we were spared. We already had a house, and we lived so far away from wartime activities that no one considered our location desirable.

We did not have a telephone at our house in Seymore, so we were hardly aware of the wartime restrictions on long-distance calls until my sister, who had come home from Arizona with her baby for a visit, had to make plans to return to her home and husband in the air force in Yuma, Arizona. Her appointed time for speaking to him on the telephone was 10:00 P.M., and the appointed place for the call was a hotel located on the square in Sulphur Springs. I begged to go along because I had never seen the interior of a hotel. We all drove to town in the truck and went directly to the hotel lobby that was, without a doubt, the most elegant place I had ever seen. I knew Mama was uncomfortable about going there because she suggested some other places we could go to make the call, but Daddy insisted that this was *the* place. Later I understood why Mama was so uncomfortable here when I learned that this was Daddy's base for his bootlegging operation. The waitresses in the cafe here evidently took orders for booze and passed them on to Daddy. Mama was probably thinking that we all might be arrested at any moment.

Puberty and War

—

BREAKING WITH TRADITION IN OUR COMMUNITY, Lola Pearl went away to college in the summer of 1942, right after high school graduation. Farm girls in our vicinity were generally expected to marry soon after high school or to become secretaries or clerks in the retail stores in town.

In light of our family's poor economic status, how could our parents afford college for their oldest child? Therein lies an interesting story that illustrates the determination and resiliency of members of my family.

Lola Pearl's high school English teacher and sponsor of the high school newspaper, Berniece Whitley, told her that she could write well and encouraged her to go to college. When the time came, Ms. Whitley offered to be her sponsor and help her find a part-time job at East Texas State Teachers College (ETSTC). Our Uncle Milty, a retail merchant in Oklahoma and only brother of our deceased maternal grandmother, agreed to pay for her tuition and books for one year and part of her room and board in the co-op system. She was to work in the library at ETSTC, and of course, she would have housekeeping duties as a co-op student.

Lola Pearl had ordered a pair of new shoes from the Sears Roe-

buck catalog, and she wore them for the first time that first day of college. She walked to the highway and caught a bus to Sulphur Springs, transferring there to another bus that took her to Commerce. She did not realize that the bus would drop her off at the college, so she got off in downtown Commerce and walked to the school. A big rainstorm came while she was walking to register, and the pasteboard soles of her shoes came unglued. She shuffled through registration, her shoes falling apart, and finally got back home, barefoot.

My sister really wanted to be a journalist not a teacher, and as a result of the war, she got a lucky break after her freshman year. The newly appointed male editor of her college newspaper decided to enlist in the U.S. Marine Corps, and the paper was left without an editor. Lola Pearl, by this time called Lola, was chosen to fill in, chiefly, she says, because there were no qualified men left around to do the job—they were all off to war. There is no doubt that the war, tragic as it was, gave women opportunities that they never would have had otherwise.

When Lola came home from college on the weekends, she showed me how to do exercises she had learned in gym class, and we tumbled in the front yard. She told me wonderful stories of dormitory life and of her new friends and showed me her books, actually taking time to explain passages to me. My sister now tells me that I was a quiet, shy child, and that she has almost no memories of me before this time.

I loved all her stories of college life, but what I liked best were stories of her boyfriends. She had not had a "real" boyfriend in high school, although the boys liked her and came around. Somehow she managed to discourage them. When a boy came to the house to call on her in her high school days, I hid in the shadows and tried to listen to their conversation. When she was in college, I read her picture postcards from soldier admirers. Because of my sister, I learned what living vicariously was long before I knew the meaning of the phrase. If she harbored dreams of becoming a war correspondent (my own fantasy), she put her dreams to rest in 1943 when she fell in love with an army air force sergeant, married him, and shortly afterward became pregnant with her first child.

While Lola was away at school, Daddy was away much of the time doing defense work, and Mama was busy trying to keep things together on the farm. This situation left me alone much of the time to

suffer teasing at the whim of my brother. Then in the summer of 1944, my brother joined my father in shipyard work in Houston. It was a long, hot summer, and somehow Mama found the courage to take me on a trip to Houston on the Trailways bus to visit my daddy and brother. We walked to the highway with our cardboard suitcase and waited for the Houston-bound bus, which we knew passed by the intersection of our dirt road and Highway 154 around four o'clock in the afternoon. As the bus driver welcomed us aboard, we paid the fare and set off together on the first trip of any distance or consequence for either of us.

When I was twelve years old and sprouting breasts, I began to walk with a stoop because I knew those two knobs would alert the world that all was not right with my body. I had had whispered conversations with Dorothy about "periods," but I did not want to admit to her that I had already started, mainly because she had not, and God knows, I did not want to be different. Something was surely wrong with me, and I must keep it a secret. When Mama saw blood on my panties one day, she said, "Oh, I meant to tell you."

And because I was too embarrassed to discuss such a thing with my mother, I answered quickly, "I already know everything."

"Who told you everything?"

"My friends," I said.

She let it go at that, probably because I was so sullen or possibly because she simply did not want to get into such a discussion. Perhaps her grandmother had never had such a discussion with her. Of course, I did not understand the first thing about what was really happening to me. We did not have a Girl Scout film telling us what to expect or even a health book outlining the female body and explaining its development. I did not have my sister there to question or confide in. She had already moved away from home, and besides, the six-year difference in our ages had seemed much greater at that time than it did later, when we were both adults.

Once settled on the bus, I sat beside Mama for the first hundred miles or so, and then I decided to sit by myself. I chose an empty seat on the other side of the aisle from her, down a few rows, toward the back of the bus. As night came on, a very flabby, pasty-looking man sat down beside me, pushing me over toward the window. I do not recall talking

to him, but as it grew darker on the bus, he somehow managed to slip his left arm underneath his right and, while looking straight ahead and without seeming to shift himself at all, he started to fondle my left breast. I scooted away until my right side was up against the wall of the bus. He had his feet stretched out, touching the back of the seat in front of him, and I saw right away that I could not escape without making a big commotion. I was paralyzed with fear as he grew bolder and started to stroke my left thigh with his right hand. I do not remember how I got away before something worse happened, but I do know that I told no one and made no noise. I guess I knew Mama would not be able to do anything about it if I told her. I guess it was for the same reason I had never told anyone that my aunt's husband had been fondling my breasts at every opportunity, even before the little buds began to blossom. Now I had something else to feel guilty about.

When we reached Daddy's boardinghouse in Houston, the first thing I did when I could manage to be alone in the bathroom that the whole floor shared was to bandage my chest tightly, mummy fashion. I was determined that no one else would see the changes going on with my body, especially not my brother, who would surely laugh at me and tell everyone my dark and terrible secret.

I loved the sights and sounds of the big city. Mr. Moore, a tall, thin man who managed the boardinghouse and cooked the meals, invited me to go with him to the grocery store to shop for food. I had never before seen the inside of a large grocery store, and I was amazed at the variety of food and the ingenuity of the packaging. The brightness of it all overwhelmed me, and the choices pushed the edges of my imagination. Mama had always made our pickles from cucumbers that she soaked in a brine mixture for days and then placed in glass jars. They were tasty, but they were always the same. Here, in this big city grocery store, there were pickles everywhere: skinny pickles, fat pickles, whole pickles, sliced pickles, spiced pickles, light green pickles, dark green pickles, bread-and-butter pickles, seven-day pickles, pickled peaches, pickled onions, and pickled pig's feet. And the cheeses! Until then, I had only eaten "rat cheese," the name we gave to cheddar. One way we dealt with poverty in East Texas was to laugh at our predicament by renaming some of our foods; for example, cream gravy became "evertime" or "poverty sop," a gravy made by pouring coffee into the hot grease left in the skillet from frying ham was called "red eye," butter was "cow salve," and peanuts were "goobers."

In Houston, the picture show down at the end of the block was another novelty. Every day I watched the marquee, waiting for just the right picture before I begged for permission to see it. As each day passed, my bound chest ached more and more. Mama became alarmed because my symptoms were so strange. Everyone was afraid of polio in those days, and she thought I might be coming down with it. For awhile I enjoyed all the attention I got from the polio scare I had caused, but then the fear that they would haul me off to the doctor made me pretend that I was suddenly feeling no pain at all. I was not about to admit that I had bound my chest so tightly I could barely breathe.

The afternoon of my "recovery" I begged for and got permission to go to the picture show. As I sat on the aisle near the back of the almost empty theater in the dark, the scales fell from my eyes. Suddenly I clearly saw that I could free myself of this misery in an instant. I started to unbutton my blouse. Right then and there, I unpinned the bandage and started to unwind it. It took forever to be free, and the whole time I was unwinding, my eyes kept darting around to see if anyone was watching me, and it appeared that I was in the clear.

Now it seems insane that I did not go to the movie house rest room to unbind myself, but I did not think of it. Public rest rooms were still sort of a novelty to me, and that could be the reason I did not think of it right away. I was also aware that when I stayed too long in the boardinghouse rest room, I was likely to be hollered at by several boarders with whom I shared the facilities. Perhaps I thought the same might be true of movie patrons, or perhaps I just did not want to miss the movie I had paid hard-won money to see.

I was free to breathe again! I was a self-imposed prisoner who had pardoned herself. I was a precursor of the sixties' bra burners before I owned a bra.

At supper that evening, my brother told me with a smirk on his face, "I saw you today at the picture show." His words wrapped around my psyche like the bandage around my chest, and I was paralyzed again, although he never said another word about it. Soon, though, it was time for Mama and me to go home, back to the farm, and I was happy to leave the city—and my brother.

Death Comes to Our House

IN NOVEMBER OF MY FIRST YEAR IN HIGH SCHOOL, near Thanksgiving, 1944, something far worse than teenage angst came down on my family. I suppose we should have seen it coming. Afterward, we never talked about whether we did or not. We never talked about those things that were painful and hidden. We just kept existing in our three separate shells, sharing a house, sorrow, and little else.

Before that awful November day, my sister had given birth to a beautiful baby girl in April. They had lived with us for a while before they joined her soldier husband, newly settled in Yuma, Arizona. While they were at our house, Daddy hired a craftsman in town to make an unusual cradle for the baby in the form of a boat. Supported by posts on either end, the little boat, the USS *Babyland,* swung all day in our front room. The baby brought a new sort of energy and joy to the house and to our family.

J. T. had come home in August from his summer shipyard job in Houston in order to begin his junior year of high school. My sister's baby brought out tenderness and gentleness in my brother that I had never seen in him before. I cherish a snapshot of my brother and first niece together that shows him standing under the sheltering limbs of the big oak tree, which still stands in front of the house, holding her,

J. T. Gammill's Sulphur Springs High School photo, circa 1944.

and looking into her face. Mama was glad to have him back. She started to smile and laugh again. He brought whistling and songs and jokes back into the house. He and Mama had a closeness that excluded me, but that was not what I minded. I was dreading the teasing that would surely follow him back into the house. There was very little of that, however. My brother had outgrown teasing and discovered nightlife. He started to go out with his friends in cars. I never knew exactly what they did on these outings, and I am sure Mama knew even less, but one thing I knew for certain: they were drinking.

One cold night he came in late, went to bed, and some hours later, in his befuddled state, mistook his shoe for the slop jar. Next morning I saw that his shoe was filled with pee. I had something to hold over *him* now, but I never had the will, or the chance, to use it.

My brother did not want to go to high school. He wanted to join the navy, and he talked about it all the time. He begged our parents to "sign" for him, to give their permission for his enlistment, but they wanted him to finish high school and would not agree to it.

"As soon as I'm seventeen, I'm joining the navy whether anybody likes it or not," he said at least once every day between September and November.

My sister and her baby had moved to their new home in Arizona by September. Daddy had quit his job in the shipyard and had come back home in October. I am not sure if this was because they no longer needed him at the shipyard or if Mama had insisted on it because she needed help with my brother. At any rate, the three of us—Mama, Daddy, and I—were all in bed asleep that November night in 1944 when the flash of car lights into the front room where I slept awakened me. Men were knocking on the door. Daddy walked sleepily through the front room to the door where the men were standing. They talked, my daddy stepped back, and strange sounds came from his throat. Then he started to sob. Mama rushed forward, toward them, clutching her nightgown. I watched from my bed, but I knew what I heard could not be so. J. T. could not be dead. He had left the house with Daddy to go to town right after supper, and there was Daddy standing right there. If Daddy was standing there, then J. T. must be in his bed, I reasoned.

As I listened, I could hear the familiar voice of an uncle who lived in town. The city police had brought the bad news to him, and he, in turn, had brought it to us. Daddy said we should get dressed and follow my uncle back to his house in town. The three of us sat in the cab of Daddy's pickup, still in shock. I was shivering as I listened to Mama and Daddy talk while we drove.

"Why didn't you bring him home with you?" Mama asked between deep sobs.

"He didn't want to come home with me. He said he just wanted to ride around with S. for awhile. And S. said he would bring him home."

"You should have paid more attention to him. If you didn't fool with that whiskey, you could have kept him with you."

"I thought he'd be all right. He wasn't drinking, and I didn't know that S. was."

Suddenly I could stand no more, and I screamed at them for the first and only time in my life, "Stop it!" There was no more talk on the way to town.

The details we learned are too painful to call up again other than in a broad sense. S., who was driving, was about fifteen years older than my brother, who was not quite sixteen. A truck loaded with steel pipe, some extending beyond the tailgate, was parked by the side of the road on the main street going into town. S. drove the passenger side of his car straight into the back of the parked truck and straight into the steel pipe that drove into my brother's heart. An eyewitness later told us that S. had jumped out of his car and pretended that J. T. had been driving.

My grief and emptiness after my brother's death were all the more intense because of the guilt I felt. Had God been listening when I said to J. T., "I hate you. I wish you was dead"? Did God know that in my heart of hearts I wished I had Dorothy's brother instead of my own because he was protective of her, always willing to fight for her, while mine was not?

Mama said, "I want his body brought home. I don't want him in that cold funeral parlor."

Some neighbor men came to sit up all night in our front room with the corpse. The fire in the fireplace turned to coals, the men drowsed, and I sneaked in, alone, to look at my only brother. Someone had put pancake makeup on his face, and he was dressed in a suit. I had never before seen him in a suit. On the third trip into the room that night, just before daybreak, I reached out to touch his hand. It was cold and hard, and I wondered why people lied and said he "looked natural." He had never worn a suit when he was alive, and he had certainly never worn pancake makeup. I wondered how it was that a person could be so whole one instant and gone the next. And where does that life go when it leaves the body behind like a discarded shell?

I do not remember a thing about his funeral, but we laid him to rest beside his baby sister, Edna Earle, in the Arbala Cemetery. Remembering how I felt then makes me realize how much greater the pain was for Mama and Daddy. This pain and the blame they laid on each other drove an even greater wedge between them.

One early morning, just about daybreak, a week after my brother died, I woke up to see him standing by my bed. He was wearing the uniform of a sailor and his white hat sat on his head at a jaunty angle. He was smiling, and in his hand he clutched a duffel bag. I sat up quickly in bed and said to him, "Oh, J. T., we thought you were dead. Everybody thought you were dead."

"Don't be silly," he answered, "I'm in the navy now."

"When did you join up?" I asked.

"Last week," he said.

I felt his physical presence so strongly, and this exchange was so real, I wanted to leap from my bed and tell someone. Something held me back. There was a simple test I could run to see if this was reality or dream before I said anything to Mama. I knew she was in the kitchen, so I sneaked to the door and peeked in. If J. T. *were* home, he would be talking to her, and she would be animated. What I saw sent me back to bed to bury my head under the covers. Through the crack in the door, I could see her back as she worked over the table making biscuits. Her shoulders were drooped, as if pulled down by the forces of gravity, and her slight frame looked heavy and tired. There was no animation about her. I had my answer.

Mama and Daddy had lost a child before. Born in the springtime of 1926, one year after Lola Pearl, the new baby, Edna Earle, died that Christmas day. Her death was sudden, too, and its reasons far less clear.

When, as a grown-up, I learned about sudden infant death syndrome, I knew instantly and with great relief that this is what had caused the baby's death. Mama and Daddy had never heard of sudden infant death syndrome. Before Mama's death, I talked to them both about what I had learned of this killer and told them I was convinced that this was what had taken their baby's life. Somehow, like so many other parents before and after them, they had lived through that awful experience of losing a child and had gone on to have two other children—my brother and me. After my brother was killed, a light went out of their eyes, and it never returned.

"Sweeping up the heart / the morning after death / is solemnest of industries / enacted upon earth" reads the poem by Emily Dickinson. And so it is.

An Alien in My
Own Country

—

I HAD ALREADY STARTED HIGH SCHOOL in September of 1944 before my brother died in November. Entering Sulphur Springs High School from my little country school was like going from nurturing parents to a foster home that already had its favored children or like going from a third world country to a more prosperous one. This experience must account for the deep empathy I still feel for immigrants in this country. Nobody told me this school was going to be so different from the one I had always known, and I did not know enough to ask.

As I look back, I see that my expectations of how something would be and the reality of the situation were often in conflict. This contradiction did not begin or end in high school, but it seems to have been more pronounced during that time.

There was a newly opened, much smaller, closer high school to the south of us—at Yantis, Texas, in Wood County—to which I could have gone. Dorothy chose to go there after that first year, and as we went our separate ways, we gradually lost contact. Freddy and the other three pupils who completed eighth grade with me also chose the nearby smaller school.

I thought the larger town school was a better school and would give me more opportunities. Besides, my sister had gone there and done well, and it was the school my brother had returned to when his

summer job in Houston was over. I knew the school, I thought, from listening to my sister and brother talk about it, but the school did not know me. My sister had already graduated when I got there, and the ice I imagined she would have broken for me stood in a solid block.

On the first day of classes in the fall of 1944, rain fell early in the morning. Half a mile of sandy road and two miles of clay road separated my house from the highway where I was to catch the school bus for the ride to town. I walked slowly, ever so carefully, avoiding the red clay mud wherever possible. When I rounded the corner leading to the last hill that led to the highway, I saw the bus waiting for me. I knew I had to catch that bus (there were no others), so I started to run. Running in slippery clay mud is like running on ice; sooner or later, one is destined to fall. And fall I did. Mud covered my new dress, the one I had been saving since summer so I could make a good impression on the first day of school. There was mud on my legs, mud on my socks, and mud on my shoes. On the first day of school, I looked like a disaster, but I did catch the school bus.

By the end of the last class on the first day of school, I could see that I was in alien territory. Most of my classmates had been in school together since first grade and had already formed tight little groups. Together they went to the drugstore for sodas after school. They went to each others' parties. Their parents, mostly town business people, socialized together. They went to church with the high school teachers and with each other, of course.

I did not know that culture shock was the term for what I was experiencing, but I did know that being different was the kiss of death. And so, I kept trying to be one of them—to be something I was not. In particular, I passionately wanted to be invited to join the one social club for girls. Their initiation rites were spectacular. On the first day of initiation, the pledges would appear at school in strange modes of dress, leaving no doubt about who had been invited to join this club and more importantly, as far as I was concerned, who had not been invited to join. On campus grounds, always in a very conspicuous place, before and after school and at lunchtime, the pledges would gather to perform the rituals demanded by their sponsoring sisters. The rest of us stood and watched at a distance. I wondered if some of the other girls standing on the sidelines with me longed to be a part of this elite group as did I. It was something we did not talk about.

Mama had let me stay home from school for a few days after J. T.'s

funeral. When I noticed that she did not pay much attention to how I looked before I left for school, I decided to wear the new navy blue crepe dress she had bought me for the funeral. After I slipped on the dress, I could tell that it seemed shorter than it had been on the day of the funeral and was stretching over my tummy. This was partly because I stooped. Convinced that I would be cuter if I were only five foot two, I went around in a perpetual stoop. (A popular song at this time went something like this, "Five feet two, eyes of blue, has anybody seen my gal?" I secretly wanted to be somebody's gal. I already had eyes of blue, and so I was certain that five foot two was the key to desirability.) As if poor posture was not enough to highlight the flaws of my body, I had been caught in the rain the last time I had worn this dress. It was cut on the bias, and it had shrunk, as that fabric has a tendency to do. We did not have a full-length mirror in which I could check my appearance, so off I went to school, forgetting about the shrinkage and thinking I looked pretty. I was deep into algebra when the person behind me tapped me on the shoulder and slipped me a note, a note I was sure had been read by everyone sitting between me and the fat boy who had written it. It said, "Who did it to you?"

I was only a freshman and had never dated—I did not even have a boyfriend—but I knew what "Who did it to you?" meant. I could think of things to say to him, things like, "You bastard," but I could not bring myself to utter them. Again I withdrew in silence and agony, feeling embarrassed about how I looked, and I did not learn another thing in algebra class.

Something else happened about this same time that made me realize how vulnerable I was right after J. T.'s death. I rode the school bus with a classmate and her little brother, Bobby. I was particularly fond of the little boy because he was wide-eyed and happy and very friendly. One morning, neither he nor his sister, my classmate, was on the bus. When I got to school, I learned that he had been hit by a truck and killed early that morning. His father had taken him to town for a haircut before school, and as they were leaving the barbershop, Bobby suddenly broke away from his father and tried to run across the street. The truck driver did not see him until it was too late. Nobody understood why I was crying uncontrollably. I did not understand it either, but I could not stop. For days I agonized over the child's death, and I could not understand my own emotions. After all,

he was not my brother. Or *was* he my brother in a larger sense? This must have been the first time I ever felt a mystical connection with another person.

J. T.'s death greatly affected the three of us—Mama, Daddy, and me—but the way in which each of us responded to the tragedy was very different. Mama withdrew more and more into the kitchen and chores. Daddy headed on an even more reckless course than before: staying out late, taking chances, selling whiskey, outrunning the sheriff, and losing his temper at the drop of a hat. I just curled up inside myself, like I used to do at the tent revivals when the preacher called me a sinner. My pain was accentuated by Daddy's behavior and the way in which he began to live his life apart from Mama and me.

My high school civics teacher announced one Monday that our class would visit the county courthouse and jail that Friday. To get out of the classroom for a field trip was something I had always enjoyed, but this announcement sent terror coursing through my veins. Daddy had not been home in a week, and we did not know where he was. I had not thought that he might be in jail though until the teacher's words filtered through to some raw nerve in my subconscious and collected there in a throbbing pool, "jail . . . to jail . . . jail." I had no doubt, then, that that was where Daddy had been for a week. My humiliation at having my classmates peer at my father through bars would be more than I could bear. I disappeared into the black hole of my outward silence.

I had a week to worry—actually from 10:30 A.M. Monday to 4:30 P.M. Thursday. I thought of nothing but the humiliation I would face. Several possible scenarios flooded my imagination. There my classmates were at the jail; I stayed home sick that day. No one recognized Daddy as he turned away when the kids walked past his cell. Just as I began to comfort myself with this thought, the next scenario flashed. There we were at the jail. Daddy was looking through the bars at us, surprised. Jean and Ann and Betty were whispering. I could not hear them, but I knew exactly what they were saying. The boys were snickering. I was weak and sick with shame. I would never be able to hold my head up again. My life was over.

So much for scenarios. On Thursday afternoon at 4:30, Daddy met the school bus at the highway. To say that I was glad to see him would be an all-time understatement. I never learned where he had been,

and I never asked. The important thing was that he was home. I do not remember if the class actually went to the jail on Friday as planned, but it did not matter anyway. By Friday, it was only a plain old field trip.

Six months after J. T. died, the war with Germany ended, and Japan's surrender came some three months after that. I saw all the wonderful end-of-war pictures in *Life* magazine. I heard on the radio inspiring stories about returning heroes and how they were welcomed home. I sat enthralled at the picture show on Saturday afternoon as newsreels of returning soldiers riding down the main streets of their hometowns flashed on the screen.

I remember all that so vividly, and yet I cannot remember any local parades or celebrations as our own soldiers, sailors, and marines returned home. Perhaps I did not have any way to get to town to see such parades. In our own extended family, we welcomed several cousins home with small get-togethers, but our greatest excitement was reserved for the return of Ben, the cousin who had been a German prisoner of war and who, when I was little, had pulled hair out of my head to stick in the head of the little devil he had molded from clay down by the spring at Arbala.

The end of the war also brought my sister, her husband, and their baby back to Texas. My brother-in-law was from Pennsylvania, so we were all relieved that he decided to look for work in Texas rather than return to his home state. They lived with us while he searched for work. He was not like the other men in our community—he was a Yankee and a Catholic—and he called me "the Belle of Hopkins County." I thought this was a particularly exciting time because they had been living far away, and I was always eager to hear about other places and people.

The end of the war meant not only the return home of the "boys" but also the return of defense workers, as they were no longer needed. Daddy came home from defense work to try farming again. Soon he was trucking fresh produce to the Dallas Farmer's Market. He never had quite a full load of vegetables from our own farm, so he would buy produce from other farmers to supplement his load. At that time, farmers who sold at the Dallas Farmer's Market had to sign an affidavit that they had raised everything they were selling there. This caused Mama some uneasy moments because she was sure every

stranger who came down the dusty road and stopped at our house was a representative from the Farmer's Market, come to check on the status of the farm. Daddy was so unconcerned about this aspect of the business that he eventually stopped trying to farm altogether and bought from other farmers everything he planned to sell at the Farmer's Market. This, too, was hard, hot, backbreaking work. Sometimes he would have to drive all over the countryside to buy, often as far away as Arkansas or Oklahoma, and sometimes he was stuck with produce he could not sell. He did not always sell at the Dallas Farmer's Market; sometimes he peddled to grocery stores and restaurants. When I was not in school, he often let me go with him on these peddling trips. He was fun to be with, and even when we had barely cleared enough money for gas, he was always ready and willing to buy me a bottle of ice-cold Coke.

My love affair with Coca-Cola had begun a few years earlier, when Daddy took me to eat at a little seating-at-the-counter-only café in Sulphur Springs—my first time ever to eat at any sort of restaurant. The cook was frying onions and hamburger patties on the grill right in front of where we sat. I had never smelled anything that made me hungrier. Pointing at the hamburgers, I told Daddy, "That's what I want." The cook slapped a patty on the grill, and I watched and listened as it sizzled. Then he toasted both sides of the bun before assembling the burger with the hot, browned patty and fried onions, lettuce, tomatoes, pickles, and mustard. Finally, he wrapped it in a thin, white paper and handed it to me. The top of the burger was glistening with grease, and the first bite made the wait worthwhile. Next, he gave me a five cent frosted bottle of ice-cold Coke. My love affair with Coke began that day, and it ended when the company switched from glass to cans and plastic bottles.

Conflicts of the Heart

⁓

I MUST HAVE BEEN ABOUT SIXTEEN when I began to identify closely with Daddy again. One part of me felt a loyalty to Mama and gratitude to her for all her sacrifices. Another part of me was ashamed of her on the rare occasions we were in town together. I thought Mama could have had new clothes once in awhile if she had insisted on it, especially when Daddy obviously had some extra money, but she stubbornly refused to do anything she considered extravagant, and that was particularly true if she suspected that the money had come from some source not absolutely upright. It was not only her appearance that bothered me, though, it was her diffidence. In the dime store or grocery store, she would wait until the clerk told her how much she owed, then timidly open her little snap pocketbook and slowly count out the cash. Daddy, under the same circumstances, would reach into his pocket, extract a roll of bills, draw off what he needed, and toss it on the counter as if there were plenty more where that came from. At sixteen, I loved this damn-the-consequences attitude in Daddy and in others and would love to have adopted it myself, but Mama's imprint on me was, and is to this day, far too powerful to allow me such indulgence.

I loved to go to town with Daddy and to be seen walking down the

sidewalk with him. He was slender, tall, and muscular. He was clean shaven and always neatly dressed. Everybody seemed to know him. Standing behind the soda fountain at the drugstore, the soda jerks would start to prepare his Bromo Seltzer. "Here comes Bromo," they would say by way of greeting. He walked with confidence; a deal maker on the move. I loved to be in the proximity of his aura.

At the same time, I realized that it was Mama who held us together as a family. She made the sacrifices. She was always there. She could be depended upon. She kept her promises, and she did not complain. Steady and stoic was Mama.

I remember once telling her that I thought Daddy treated her unfairly. "Leave him," I said. "I'll get a job at Duke & Ayers and support us." (Duke & Ayers was a dime store with sloping wooden floors on the town square in Sulphur Springs.)

Out of touch with reality? Had I been able to get a job at the dime store in town and had it paid as much as fifty cents an hour, how could I have gotten there? Walked twelve miles? Sensibly, she said. "We'll manage."

Daddy's stories at this time were exhilarating, though seldom repeatable. I remember overhearing him tell his friend, Bruce, a story about an incident that had occurred late the previous evening. He had been on his way home from Dallas, where he had gone to buy whiskey and beer to resell. Driving south from Sulphur Springs on Highway 154 toward home, he had heard a siren and had seen flashing lights in his rearview mirror. The hour was late, and he had thought his nemesis, Bear Tracks, would surely be asleep in bed. He accelerated, "floorboarded," he said, and noticed that the speedometer had reached its limit. He had been holding the steering wheel with one hand and throwing bottles out the window with the other.

Bruce was laughing and slapping his knees. Daddy was enjoying telling his story as much as Bruce was listening to it. As for me, the eavesdropper, I felt excited by these stories because they injected some life from the outside world into our humdrum existence. At the same time, I was highly embarrassed by some of the things Daddy said and did.

I went through a period of wanting to know the men with whom Daddy associated. Once, I had talked to one of them when I was in town without my father. I repeated the conversation at supper, sometime later, probably embellishing it, and Daddy let me know with just

a look that I had better avoid any further contact with any of his male acquaintances. So I did.

Strangely, unlike the sharp images I have of my very early childhood, I have less vivid memories of my high school life. I am sure that some of this lack of recollection has to do with those years being so painful. I can now see that those years were painful chiefly because I was trying so hard to fit in with the popular kids that I continued to set myself up for disappointments.

During my junior or senior year in high school, someone's discarded piano wound up in our front room—maybe it was payment to Daddy for a gambling debt or a whiskey bill. It was boxy, heavy, and took up a lot of space in the small room. Mama was not happy about having something that was of no use to anyone, so I took advantage of her practicality and begged for permission and money to take piano lessons. I dreamed of being able to play the piano and sing like Daddy's sister, Aunt Lola. These talents surely would make me popular.

Mama finally agreed that I could take lessons if I could find a piano teacher and find a ride home from school, because I would surely miss the school bus, which left promptly at 4:00 P.M. I inquired around and learned that my popular town classmates were taking lessons from Mrs. Gomer Wilson, who lived not far from school. One day during my lunch hour, I walked over to her house and told her what I wanted to do. She was very kind and encouraging. She even rearranged her own schedule so that I could come for my lesson during an off period and be back at school before the bus left. I think she liked the fact that I had enough spunk to negotiate and arrange for lessons on my own. What I had not counted on was a public recital. I knew the dictionary definition of the word recital, but I did not know what a small town piano recital was. After a few months of giving me lessons, Mrs. Wilson told me that she wanted me to participate in her next student recital. I did not want to tell her that I had no evening dress, so I borrowed one from a classmate who had several. I practiced my piece, "Turkey in the Straw," until I knew it backward and forward. Mama and Daddy received a handwritten invitation to the recital. Mama was in the audience, surely uncomfortable in Mrs. Wilson's formal living room, with the town mothers who all knew each other. She sat quietly and dignified in her aloneness, responding politely when spoken to. We "pianists" were in Mrs. Wilson's kitchen

and screened-in back porch listening to each piece and awaiting our turns. As I listened, I realized that I was outclassed. These kids were good. Of course, most of them had been taking lessons since they were seven years old, and recitals were already old hat to them. I became uneasy and uncomfortable in the borrowed dress. I felt like an impostor. By the time Mrs. Wilson announced my number, I was weak with fear. Had Mama not been in the audience, I would have run out the back door, but I could not bear to make her ashamed of me or to leave her there alone. I remember getting through the piece without ever hearing the notes I was playing. I felt like a complete failure although the applause was polite (as it was for everyone), and none of the other students laughed at me, at least not openly, as I had feared they might. My dreams of playing piano like my Aunt Lola ended there as did my dreams of singing like her when I joined the high school chorus.

Living in the country without the convenience of a telephone or transportation made dating difficult. If a boy wanted to take me out, he could not call. He had to drive to my house and ask me out, and I, in turn, then had to get permission from Mama. If she said yes, he had to wait while I got dressed. It was awkward, and I suppose it is no small wonder that I dated very few of my high school classmates. I did not even have a date for the junior/senior banquet or the senior dance. I remember going to one of these affairs with some other girls without escorts, but I felt terribly self-conscious, and it was not much fun for me.

Once, I was asked out by a popular classmate on whom I had a crush (popular chiefly because he was a good piano player). We had made the date at school for the following Saturday night. I had given him directions to the farm. He drove the thirteen miles out and picked me up to go to the show in town. Immediately after the show, he drove me home without even first offering to buy me a Coke. We sat in his car talking for a few minutes. There in the country with no electric lights to interfere with its glow, the moon loomed so large and low, it seemed touchable, creating a perfect atmosphere on this clear and chilly autumn night. The stars seemed to dance around the moon. I felt romance in the air. Evidently he did not, and very soon afterward he drove away, saying nothing about wanting to see me again. I could only conclude that he had suffered his own culture shock when he

saw where I lived—so unlike anything he was accustomed to. Either it was that, I decided, or he had only asked me out on some foolish dare.

On this particular evening, no one was home. Mama rarely left the house at night, but this evening she had gone with Daddy to visit a cousin nearby. I went into the empty house and started to search the kitchen for something to eat. I found a jar of fresh cream Mama had been saving to make butter. I whipped it, added plenty of sugar, and sat there in the kitchen trying to soothe the pain of my most recent disappointment while I devoured the whole bowl of whipped cream.

I did have a few boyfriends who also lived in the country, but I knew that I did not want to marry anyone from my community or nearby for fear that I would be stuck there forever in the same rut. This was not long after World War II ended. My head was still filled with images of women war correspondents, women in the military, and women in crisp, white nurse's uniforms. Women could do something besides stay home, but how I could get from here to there, I had no real clue.

I do not recall when I began to have such high expectations for myself—high expectations without any real grasp of what it would take to bring them to fruition. I do remember that as a small child, I began to keep my desire for recognition a very private matter. The closer I held these desires to my heart, the more exaggerated they became. I always had opinions, but I seldom voiced them. I always knew I was smart, but the fear that I might be wrong—and ridiculed for being so—was, at times, overpowering. I would succeed, but I would do it quietly just in case I failed.

I was accepted into the National Honor Society in high school and was very proud of this honor, which was based on grades and involvement in class activities and not on popularity, as was student council membership (which I had longed for but for which I was never chosen). I talked very little to my family about my many disappointments in high school, but they knew how important the National Honor Society was and went all out to help me. Mama and I went to town and bought a beautiful aqua suit in a dressy fabric for the initiation ceremony. The long-sleeved blouse had gold buttons down the front, and the skirt was fully pleated. I still do not know how she managed to get the money together to buy that outfit. I can

imagine her taking a handkerchief from her purse, untying the knot where she had secured the money, and handing the cash to the clerk.

Both Mama and Daddy came to the initiation ceremony. My happiness in this triumph was rather short-lived though. I knew that I had a required course, plane geometry, coming up the next fall that would cause me trouble. Only one teacher taught this course, and she was the only teacher in the whole school I disliked intensely. I learned that some students avoided this teacher by taking the course in summer school. I begged Mama to let me share a rental room in town with two other girls so that I could go to summer school and get that awful course behind me, but she would not agree to it. Aside from Mama's objection to the cost, she surely knew I was not mature enough to live away from home, even for a short time.

I had expected to do badly in the course when I took it the next fall, and I did. This brought my grade average down, and I was dropped from the National Honor Society—a genuine humiliation for me.

I was on the high school newspaper staff during my junior and senior years, but I could never stay for after-school meetings because I had no transportation home if I missed the school bus, which left promptly at 4:00 P.M. For the same reason, I could not attend high school football games, not even home games. For really special occasions, I sometimes spent the night in town with my aunt or a girl-friend.

I used to think: life just has to get better for me; if I can hold on, my life will change. I never wanted to kill myself no matter how badly I thought things looked. Now I can see that I must have absorbed some of Mama's patience in adversity and some of Daddy's ability to bounce back after being knocked down.

Happily, my life did change for the better, starting with the last couple of months of high school. I felt important at high school graduation. Although I did not win any special honors or go to any great parties, I was going away to college, and I had a boyfriend who had come all the way from Texarkana on the bus to be present for my graduation ceremonies. His name was Emanuel, and he thought I was beautiful. He thought so even after we had to ride in the back of Daddy's pickup following graduation and after he had to use our old outhouse because we still had no indoor bathroom or running water.

I had met Emanuel on a bus when I was returning home from a

short visit to a cousin's house in South Texas a couple of months before high school graduation. I think he fell in love with me almost instantly, and I was in love with the idea of having a boyfriend. He was a handsome young man despite having lost an eye in a childhood accident. He wore a very natural appearing glass eye, but he did not drive. When he later came to my college to visit me, I was embarrassed to have to meet him at the bus station and walk everywhere we went. Eventually, he gave up, and I wonder sometimes even now if he ever realized how lucky he was to be free of the shallow, immature person I was then.

The summer after graduation from high school in 1948, I went by bus to visit my sister, who had moved with her husband and small children to Pittsburgh, Pennsylvania. It was the first time I had ever taken a long trip by myself and the first time I had ever been away from home for very long. Texas was beginning to turn brown when I left, so I marveled at the green loveliness of the Pennsylvania countryside.

I loved being on my own. I bought a pair of red high heels with some of my graduation money, and I flirted shamelessly that summer with every boy I met. I was so full of myself—so sure that my life was going to be one long, exciting adventure from that moment on.

I clearly remember one incident from this time, more puzzling than dark or light. A husband and wife who lived upstairs from my sister offered to take me sightseeing since she was busy at home taking care of small children. Before this trip, I had never spent a night in a large city and had never seen a factory, a large department store, an elevator, or a major league baseball game. When this couple invited me to go to a Pittsburgh Pirates game with them, I was too excited for words. Now I would actually see these great players I had only heard about. I did enjoy seeing the game, but I do not remember who they played or who won. What I do clearly remember is the exchange that took place between the husband of the couple treating me to this great outing and myself:

"What do you people down in Texas think about the race situation?"

"What situation? I don't know what you're talking about?"

He proceeded to spell it out for me: races should be kept in their proper places; Texans knew how to do that.

It was obvious to me that he did not like blacks, but I certainly did not read his remarks as a compliment either to Texas or to me. I remember thinking, you are the racist—not me. Remember, this was 1948. Not until I finished college and moved to Chicago to live in 1951 did I begin to see more clearly whence I had come.

Leaving East Texas

DURING THE WAR, MANY OF OUR NEIGHBORS had moved their families from farms to cities where there was work to support the war effort. Having already established themselves in more populated areas during the war, they stayed on afterward and found other work there. Those who had not moved away, like my family, found themselves in much the same situation they had been in before the war—stuck on a hardscrabble farm. Although Daddy had made more money working at common labor on defense jobs during the war than he had ever made before, he still had no spare money to put aside for his children's education.

In today's world, going to college seems a natural next step. Most young people simply take for granted that going to college is the next thing they are supposed to do, especially since nearby community colleges make it affordable, and cars make it accessible. In our small East Texas community, going away to school was still a bit of a rarity in 1948, but Mama had set a precedent for my sister and me. She had gone from elementary school to what she referred to as "subcollege" in the early years of the 1920s. With a loan from the same uncle who had helped Mama go away to school and the promise of a part-time

job in the library, my sister had gone away to East Texas State Teachers College after her graduation from high school in 1942.

In 1948, during the last months of my senior year in high school, I began to think about the options open to me after graduation. If scholarships, grants, and federal loans were available in those days, I knew nothing of them. I knew that some scholarships were available to the highest-ranking students in the class and that some of the town service organizations granted a few to certain students, but those were unavailable to me. I could work in town (if I could find a job and if I could find transportation to and from that job), or I could, perhaps, borrow money from the same uncle who had helped my mother and sister go to teachers' college, but I knew for certain, then, that I did not want to be a teacher. I could go to nursing school, I told Mama, but she wondered aloud how I could possibly consider that since I could not stand the sight of blood and cringed at the thought of emptying a slop jar, which was not all that unlike emptying the bedpan of a sick patient. Then maybe, I countered, I could go to telegraph school in Springfield, Missouri (or was it Springfield, Illinois), with my friend. We could get jobs and work our way through school. "Ooh," Mama said, "too far away to think about."

Around this time, three young women, all former students from our high school, came to talk to our senior girls about the joys of attending Texas State College for Women (TSCW) in Denton. I had not heard of that school before, but it did not have "teacher" in its title. I became excited when I learned of the possibilities for different majors. I would not have to be a teacher! Denton was farther away from the farm than Commerce, but it, too, had a cooperative plan whereby a student living in the Smith Carroll system could pay for about half of her room and board fees by working in the kitchen or cleaning the dormitory for one hour each day. Textbooks could be rented and turned in at the end of the year. Spending money could be earned by working odd jobs around the campus, and by today's standards, the tuition fees were minuscule. One of the girls gave me a TSCW catalog.

For weeks I thumbed through that 1948 pamphlet until it was worn, spinning stories around each picture, just as I had spun romantic stories around the pictures of glamorous stars in the old movie magazines I had worn thin.

Recently, in preparation for my fiftieth college reunion at TSCW, now know as Texas Woman's University (TWU), I came across that same old college catalog and yellowed letters from the registrar's office responding to my inquiries about enrolling there. Among this old correspondence, I found a receipt for two dollars documenting the "Co-operative Room Assurance Fee for the 1948 Summer Session." What could two dollars reserve today?

Other summer sessions charges outlined in one of the letters from the registrar read, "Tuition for Texas Students: $15.00; Laboratory, medical, textbook and student activities fees: $4.00; Room and Board (estimated): $29.50. . . . This rate is figured for each term of the summer session and is to be paid at the time of registration for each term: June 2 and July 15, 1948." So, for a little less than one hundred dollars, I was able to attend summer school for two semesters.

Regular session expenses for 1948–49 broke down as follows for a total of $234 per semester: tuition: $50; laboratory and other fees: $30; room and board: $154. In light of today's emphasis on political correctness, one paragraph in a handout entitled "General Information for Students Living in the Smith Carroll System" seems particularly jarring, "Students who are physically handicapped and unable to participate in the housekeeping duties in the dormitories cannot be accepted in the System."

When I was seventeen, those facts and figures only meant that I would have a substantial argument to support my romantic notion of leaving home. I wrote to my uncle, telling him what I wanted to do and asking for a loan. He agreed to send me some money. Now, I only had to convince my folks that I really needed to go all the way to Denton to go to school. It would not be too hard to bring Mama around to my side. After all, I had already planted the idea that some girls were going as far away as Springfield—wherever that was.

I practiced the argument I would present to Daddy, figuring that he would not have a very strong counter since I had heard him say more than once over the years, "A girl should have a good education, because if her husband should die, she can make a living for herself and her children by teaching school." I was careful to avoid mentioning my aversion to teaching, leaving out of my argument the fantasy and emphasizing the economy. I would major in journalism, I told him, secretly seeing myself as a war correspondent in mysterious

places, even though the war had been over for three years. "Well, get your teaching certificate just in case you need it," he admonished, and I was not about to argue.

We loaded my few belongings into the back of the pickup truck and the three of us—Mama, Daddy, and I—drove to Denton. Daddy drove the pickup, sideboards rattling, into the shady lane just off Bell Avenue, which cut through the campus of Texas State College for Women, and pulled up in front of a two-story white frame building with "LAMAR HALL" painted over the front door. Girls were walking out, laughing, and talking. My first impulse was to be ashamed that I was making my grand entrance to my new life riding in an old pickup flecked with mud and manure and accompanied by totally unsophisticated parents. If I had imagined I would arrive in such a manner in full view of the people I would be living with for the next four years, I am sure I would never have had the courage to begin college. But then, thinking ahead and facing reality were never my strong suits.

"Are you a freshman?" one of the girls asked me.

"Yes."

"Then hurry. We're on our way to take a test for freshmen. We'll wait for you here."

The first words spoken to me in my new college life were words of inclusion!

I had brought only one small pasteboard suitcase; a cardboard box containing some towels, two sheets, and a blanket; and a paper sack full of the odds and ends I had collected during my first seventeen years of life. The three of us easily carried all of my belongings upstairs in one trip. Daddy, walking behind Mama and me, had my few dresses and one coat draped over his arm. As we started up the stairs, someone yelled, "Man on second!" (Later, I was to become familiar with this phrase that I had never heard before.) When we opened the door to room nine, it was obvious that my roommate, now somewhere else on campus, had already moved in and claimed the single bed nearest the only window.

Placing all my belongings on the bottom half of the bunk bed near the door to the hall, we hurried back outside so I could join those other freshmen walking across the campus to take "the test." I looked back to see Daddy and Mama pulling away in the truck. Now I was

on my own for the first time in my life. I would not have to worry about Mama's worrying about Daddy's activities. Now I would have an indoor toilet, a real bathtub, and access to a telephone. From now on, my worries would stem from my own transgressions and short-comings, of which, of course, at this time, I was blissfully ignorant.

EPILOGUE

As I come to the end of this story, I see that the fullness of a life journey—the influences which shape it, its own shaping influences, and the impact of time and place on it—can scarcely be imagined in the beginning.

The old house at Arbala is gone now, as are most of the people who once lived in it. The post office is gone, as is the cotton gin, blacksmith shop, general store, and the school. The young men no longer sit around the old store playing dominoes or pitching horseshoes on Sunday mornings while their wives stay home and cook dinner or go to Sunday school.

The one common meeting place they all now enjoy is the community center. Along with other activities held there, they have dances. I do not know how today's young people of Arbala and surrounding communities feel about having a place to socialize and dance, but I do know that as a teenager, my heart would have quickened at the thought of a nearby place to dance. When Mama and Daddy were young, house dances were popular; but when I was young, there were no nearby dances. In this particular center, the senior citizen dances are the most popular with both the musicians and dancers being "up in age."

In one respect, the Seymore community seems to have changed little since I left. The home place is still in our family. I often go there to walk in the woods, to smell the freshness of the country, and to feel young again. My sister lives in the "new" house, the one our uncle and his son, with Daddy's help, built sixty years ago. The old dirt road leading to the house is now paved. The building in which I started first grade still stands, its outdoor privy is still used. Although it has

not served as a school for more than half a century, it is sometimes used as an occasional meeting place. Our school reunions have been held there, but since "school closings" are no longer a way of life, the wonderful smells of bubbling Hopkins County Stew wafting from big, black wash pots over open fires are now only a memory. Nearby on Highway 154, one finds a general store, an air-conditioning business, and a popular barbecue restaurant. As in Arbala, about half the community consists of senior citizens, though more young families are moving in. Now, of course, everyone has a car and access to a larger world.

If Mama's life changed much after I went away to school, I was not aware of it. She still worked on the farm, methodically and steadily, day in and day out, even if there were no more children to take care of. Around 1955 she finally got running water in the house. To have a bathroom with a flushing toilet and hot water for baths was truly a luxury. She no longer had to heat the water for dish washing. About this time she got a modern refrigerator and a store-sized freezer. She had replaced the old wood cookstove with a gas stove as soon as butane gas became available to them. Years before, she had replaced the heavy black irons with an electric iron. Even with all these labor-saving devices, Mama still worked from daylight to dark.

For several years after I had married and left home, Daddy tried to establish several small businesses: he raised quail to sell to restaurants, took over a lease on a cafe in West Texas, and raised chickens. In all these enterprises, Mama pitched right in whether she liked what they were doing or not. After some disappointments in these new ventures, they came back to the farm, where Mama was more comfortable, and once more began to raise produce and collect eggs from their chickens to sell at the Dallas Farmer's Market.

Both Mama and Daddy continued to work hard long after some of their contemporaries were already, at least occasionally, enjoying retirement. Daddy was in poor health when he retired, a few years after reaching sixty-five. He tore down the chicken houses, sold the chickens, turned his farmland into pasture, and began to phase out his various small enterprises, such as cutting and selling wood. Now he and Mama seemed to be settling into a slightly more contented, happier way of life. They did more things together. The antagonism between them seemed to diminish. Mama's chief disappointment at this

time was that Daddy would not let her keep a milk cow. Daddy claimed that keeping a cow would make too much work for her.

Daddy had been hospitalized many times over the years; Mama never was. He fully expected to die before she did; he did not. Around 1978 she had a stroke, and my sister took both of our parents to live with her family in Irving for several months until Mama gained enough strength to go home. To our surprise, Daddy became a loving nurse for Mama. She recovered from that illness and lived until June of 1981. I think their last years were their best in terms of their relationship with each other.

I do not know how long Daddy could have lived without Mama or what the quality of his life would have been had my sister not moved in with him. Since Daddy had such an abhorrence of nursing homes and an irrational fear of being constrained (which he was certain would happen to him if he ever had to be a resident of one), he and my sister agreed that her moving in with him would be the best thing to do. Her husband had died earlier that year and her children were grown and on their own.

Daddy died sitting in his easy chair, just a few feet away from where my sister was preparing lunch for them. He made no noise, and she did not know he had slipped away until she called him for the meal. He had outlived Mama by five years.

At the same time my sister was looking out for Daddy, she went back to college, commuting between the farm and East Texas State University (ETSU), where she had started college all those years earlier.

She has seven children, seventeen grandchildren, and eight great-grandchildren. She lives on the old home place in Seymore, gardens, reads voraciously, sews, writes letters, looks after the livestock, and enjoys living in the country. I call her "the Cattle Baroness" and tease her that next year she will be invited to the prestigious Cattle Barons' Ball in Dallas. She could be certain, I tell her, that she would be the only genuine cow puncher there. She could drive up in Daddy's old pickup, hay clinging to the tires, and lend some authenticity to that socially elite gathering.

As for me, how do I sum up that half century since Mama and Daddy dropped me off in Denton to start college? I could begin by saying that college was a better fit than high school. Three years after Mama and Daddy brought me to college for the first time, they re-

turned for my graduation and were as proud as any parents there. A young man I had met in Indiana in the summer of 1949, when I had gone to live with my parents while Daddy had helped to build a gas pipeline from Texas northward, also came to my graduation. We had been corresponding and visiting back and forth for two years, so I do not think my folks were completely surprised when, a few days after my graduation, Marty Cimarolli told Daddy that he wanted to marry me and take me to Chicago to live.

On the day I left home, I remember sitting on the front steps with Daddy, and he started to cry. Embarrassed by his tears, he started to tease me, "If you marry an Eye-talian and move to Chicago, you'll be eating spaghetti three times a day!" We both laughed.

Marrying into an extended ethnic family and moving into their large urban community was a real eye-opener for me. I soon went to work in Chicago's Loop for a publisher of law journals. I immediately loved the city, my job, and the new friends I made. In Chicago, there were wonderful stores like Marshall Field's, where I soon learned I could just browse through without apology, and great bookstores I could lose myself in during lunch hour without explaining that I just wanted to look. For the first time I realized I could buy a book that I did not actually *need*. I also experienced my first ride on a commuter train to downtown Chicago from our community of Roseland on the far south side, my first ride in a taxicab, and my introduction to the great museums, particularly the Chicago Art Institute. All the firsts now blend into one glorious memory.

Learning to become a genuine part of the Cimarolli family took more time. The first year, Marty and I moved into our own small apartment in the community where his family lived. The second year, Marty and his father added an upstairs flat to their family home for us. His mother and father lived in the basement flat, his sister and her family on the first floor, the two of us on the second, and his other sisters lived nearby. Despite all that closeness, I still cherish them as family, although we are now separated by many miles.

Marty died suddenly in 1967. Our children, James Tice and Maria Kathryn, were nine and twelve years old. At the end of that school year, my children and I moved to Texas to be near my family. I was thirty-seven years old and living within ten miles of where I had grown up. I was starting over again, this time with a much heavier heart.

The summer after our return to Texas, my son and I worked for Daddy in the fields and at the Dallas Farmer's Market. The experience of working all day in the hot fields, rising at 4:00 A.M. to get the vegetables to market a hundred miles away, and sleeping in the back of the truck on pallets if we did not sell out during the day wore thin very quickly, so I decided to go back to graduate school the next fall. I reminded myself of the country preacher I knew when I was a child who, while toiling in the hot fields, suddenly heard the voice of the Lord calling him. He threw down his hoe, gave up farming forever, and became a preacher. I did not hear the voice of the Lord, but I did throw down the hoe, give up farming forever, and become a teacher, in spite of all that early scheming to avoid it.

I decided that teaching was the life for me after all when I discovered one day early in my career that no matter how I felt when I left for school in the morning, I always felt better and more alive when I interacted with my students throughout the day. I spent the last twenty years of my career teaching English at a community college in Dallas. I remarried in 1977.

None of us chooses the families we are born into or the times and places of our growing up, yet we are often marked for life by those accidentals. Growing up in the thirties and forties of the depression and World War II colored my way of looking at life more through light and shadow than through darkness. Growing up in the depression taught me something about the difference between need and luxury. Growing up in rural East Texas taught me about the wonders and beauty of unspoiled places and of the random cruelties of nature. During World War II, I learned something about the dual nature of man and about the cruelties we humans too often inflict upon one another. Growing up in this family assigned to me by fate taught me early on about resilience, unconditional love, the healing power of sacrifice and patience, and the randomness of life itself, in particular, my opportunity to experience life's highs and lows while my baby sister and teen brother never truly lived.

It seems to me that the family of man changes little from age to age; but I do believe that certain times and places leave a mark on a whole generation. To me, those of us who had a 1930's childhood and a 1940's adolescence have at least this in common: a deep respect for hard work, an ability to make do with what we have and get up after

being knocked down, and an appreciation for small pleasures. Contemporary wages and prices seem almost obscene to those of us who worked a month in the thirties and forties for what an hour or two of work now brings in the marketplace. Many of us view the good-times bubble with a certain suspicion and still pick up pennies from the walkways.

I come away from this labor of love with a better understanding of the conflicts within my own heart, a deeper awareness of the legacy my East Texas farm family left me, and an even deeper appreciation for the gift of life itself. I hope others will come away from this book with a better understanding of how the history and politics of this time and place, so familiar to many from textbook study, played themselves out in the minds and hearts of one East Texas farm family, who struggled through, yet survived the hardest of times in the first half of the twentieth century.

INDEX

Arbala, community of, 5–18, 42, 54, 55, 60, 61, 163
Arizona, Daddy's brief stay in, 109–13, 117
automobile, first sighting of, 42

bartering, 30–33
"Bear Tracks" (county sheriff), 36–39
benefactor, "Uncle Milty" Cates, 49, 134, 158, 160
Birch Creek Bottom, 10–12, 81, 82
blacksmith shop, 22
boiled custard, 13
Bonanza, community of, 46, 48–50
bootlegging, 35–39
building the new house, 64–68

Carnation Milk Plant, 110
Cemetery Day, 88–91
church: Arbala Community, 8–10; Seymore Community, 22
cigarettes, rolling your own, 9–10
cotton: ginning, 80, 81; picking, 79, 80
Cotton Stamps, 92–95

Dallas Farmers Market, 148, 167
Depression, Great, 5, 19, 20–119

East Texas State Teachers College, 53, 134, 135, 165

Edward VII, 3
electricity, 114–16

grandparents: maternal, 46–51; paternal, 5–9, 40–50
graveyard working. See Cemetery Day
Gray, Thomas, 3

hitchhiking, 132
Hitler, Adolph, 5
hog-killing day, 24–26
home remedies, 104–108
homecoming. See Cemetery Day
honey, harvesting, 15
Hoover, Herbert, 5
Hopkins County Stew, 27, 76

Johnson's Ice Cream Parlour, 96, 109

Kaiser, Wilhelm II, 3
Kerosene, 65; cookstove, 65; lamps, 15, 35, 36, 114, 115
Ku Klux Klan, 103

Lenin, Nicolai, 3

Mother's Day, 7, 8

"Old Age Pension," 45
Old Settler's Reunion, 86–88

patent medicines, 107; Black Draught, 12, 107

peddler. *See* Watkins man

politics: elected county officials, 98; Jim Hogg, 101; John Nance Garner, 101; Ma and Pa Ferguson, 100; Sam Rayburn, 101, 102; W. Lee (Pappy) O'Daniel, 101; "Yellow-Dog" Democrats, 98

poll tax, 99

Prohibition, 99

racism, 102, 103

radio, 116, 120, 121

railroading in Sweetwater, 55–60

REA. *See* electricity

"Relief," 109

religious revival meetings, 82–86

Repeal, consequences of, 99

Roosevelt, Franklin D., 5, 92, 93, 101, 115; New Deal, 36, 92; cotton stamps, 92–95; REA, 114–16

Roosevelt, Theodore, 3

Rural Electric Administration (REA). *See* electricity

school: "big room," 24, 124–27; closing ceremonies, 75–77; first teacher, 74, 75; first visit, 23, 24; high school, 144–48; "little room," 24, 72–79

Seymore (East Texas) community, 20–34, 64–68, 72–86, 118

Shivarees, 60, 61

snow ice cream, 22

snuff, family use of, 8

song titles and/or short excerpts from: "Dapple Gray," 18; "I Love To Tell The Story," 85; "Poor Babes In The Woods," 18; "Pretty Red Wing," 68; "Put Your Little Foot," 68, 77; "Softly And Tenderly, Jesus is . . . ," 84; "Where He Leads Me . . . ," 85

strawberry picking, 82

Sweetwater, Texas, 55–61

syrup making, 30, 31, 32

Tennessee, Gammill exodus, 40, 41

Texas State College For Women, 159–62

tobacco, smoking, 9

typhoid fever, 28–30

wagon shed, as a dwelling, 64–68

wash pot, various uses, 27, 28

Watkins man (peddler), 32–34

Women's Suffrage, 99

wood cutting, 31, 32

World War I, 57

World War II: convoys of U.S. soldiers, 122; defense work, 123; draft, 123–24; glamour of war, 124; military service, 123, 124; Pearl Harbor, 120; radio commentators, 121; radio for our schoolroom, 127; rationing, 128–33; "Stars and Stripes," 121; travel bureau, 131; war bond rallies, 122